Pornography, Feminism and the Individual

Pornography, Feminism and the Individual

ALISON ASSITER

PLUTO  PRESS

London • Concord, Mass

First published 1989 by Pluto Press
345 Archway Road, London N6 5AA
and 141 Old Bedford Road,
Concord, MA 01742, USA

Reprinted 1991

British Library Cataloguing-in-Publication Data
Assiter, Alison.
  Pornography, feminism and the individual
  1. Pornography. Social aspects
  I. Title
  363.4'7

  0–7453–0319–6
  0–7453–0521–0 pbk

Library of Congress Cataloging-in-Publication Data
Assiter, Alison
  Pornography, feminism and the individual/Alison Assiter.
      p. cm
  Bibliography: p.
  Includes index.
  ISBN 0–7453–0319–6
  ISBN 0–7453–0521–0 (pbk.)
    I. Pornography–Social aspects. 2. Feminism. 3. Dworkin,
Andrea–Views on pornography. 4. Autonomy (Psychology)
5. Liberalism.
I. Title
HQ471.A85 1989
363.4'7–dc20
                                                    89-8632
                                                    CIP

Printed and bound in the UK by Billing and Sons Ltd, Worcester

Contents

To Ben

Acknowledgements

This book has gone through a great many variations, and I am indebted to a large number of people for helpful comments. In particular, I would like to thank Richard Kuper, Anne Phillips, Keith Graham, Pat East, Diana Adlam, Robert East, Tina Chanter, Anne Beech at Pluto, Sarah Stewart, who copyedited the manuscript; the Woman and Philosophy collective, and several groups of students on the Gender and Society Course at Thames Polytechnic.

I must also thank my friend Valerie Osborne, for her untiring patience in deciphering my dreadful handwriting. A special thank you goes to Cyril who not only deciphered my handwriting but tended to my material needs (mostly for food) during the writing of this book.

Introduction

In recent years we have seen a spate of new books about pornography. These texts are largely, though not exclusively, of two types: liberal and radical feminist. The liberal tomes were mostly written in the 1960s, when several court cases were held in the USA and Britain to remove bans on the import and sale of books, including *Fanny Hill*, *Lady Chatterley's Lover* and Henry Miller's *Tropic of Cancer*. Writers, critics and judges of the time sought to remove bans on these works on the grounds that they constituted art. Artistic works, it was argued, differed from pornographic publications in that they 'discharged emotion' as part of the artistic enterprise.[1] People should not be reduced to the absurdity of hiding in their clothing the books they had purchased in Paris in order to get them through US customs; they should be able to buy them across the counter. Some liberals went even further, arguing that the distinction between literature in which sex figured largely and pornography, in which sex was the central point, was disingenuous. Kenneth Tynan, for instance, claimed that porno-graphy, while intended to be sexually arousing, could be art. *Fanny Hill*, he said, was 'expertly titillating'.[2]

Radical feminist writing came to the fore in the late 1970s and early 1980s. The authors argued that male violence was at the root of women's subordination, and that pornography was the epitome of male power. Heterosexual sex was seen as essentially violent; the penis was the symbol of violence. Following the publication of Andrea Dworkin's *Pornography: Men Possessing Women*, many radical feminists in the USA and Britain went on the campaigning trail. Women Against Violence Against Women (WAVAW) groups smashed the windows of porn shops and advocated the banning of pornographic movies. Activists in the USA and Canada sought (successfully in several cases) to have several publications – those that violated women's civil rights – exempted from the protection of the First Amendment.

On the face of it, the wheel had come full circle. Twenty years earlier, liberal opponents of censorship fought the restrictions of the state and its moralistic backers, who so feared the 'depravity' of pornography and its 'obscene, lewd, lascivious and indecent' content. Now radical feminists were advocating the banning of porn, and it looked very much as though they were following in the footsteps of the moralists of the 1960s. As with the nineteenth-century campaign against prostitution,[3] it was easy for the two standpoints to be seen as one. Their immediate aim – the banning of porn – was the same, but where one objected to the tendency of pornography to 'corrupt the mind', the other protested the degradation of women.

In fact the real commonality is between the liberals and the radical feminists. If we ignore their hoped-for results for the moment, and look instead at motivation and underlying principles, we can see this clearly. Liberals are committed to certain values: freedom, individualism and autonomy. Some of these values are worthy and should be upheld. But their defence requires a different perspective from that of their reprobate cousin, individualism. And it is precisely that individualism which many radical feminists share with their erstwhile opponents. Andrea Dworkin, for instance, is committed to a focus on the self and self-interest. Almost despite themselves, I argue in this book, many of the radical feminists of the 1980s are immersed in the individualist tradition. Though radical feminists are right to criticise porn, part of the content of their critique, I argue, is misguided.

In the first four chapters of the book, my argument is philosophical in tone, although many philosophers may regard it as sketchy. It is not so much directed towards philosophers as towards a general readership and towards those individualists whose values this book sets out to counter. In Chapter 1, I discuss the notion of freedom of speech, and link it with the wider liberal values of liberty and autonomy. In Chapter 2, I look at the notions of the 'public' and the 'private'. Chapter 3 examines various forms of individualism; Chapter 4 discusses autonomy. I argue in these first four chapters that the values of liberty and autonomy should be defended, but that such a defence requires that one moves away from the individualist outlook.

In the following four chapters I look at the views of three influential radical feminists: Andrea Dworkin, Susan Griffin and Susanne Kappeler (although I also discuss other feminist writings). I argue that each thinker, to differing degrees, remains caught in the individualist tradition. Andrea Dworkin, I suggest, is committed to an individualist outlook and to the focus on the self and self-interest which goes along with that perspective. Many of the values she upholds either explicitly or implicitly, I argue, imply that she denigrates and often scorns 'ordinary' women who remain trapped in 'patriarchal' ideology.

Susan Griffin is immersed in the individualist tradition in a different way. A central difficulty with her writing is that her Freudian focus on the relationship between mother and son becomes an ahistorical examination of those individuals, abstracting them from their family and social context. The third radical feminist, Susanne Kappeler, is dedicated to the destruction of individualism. Yet, despite herself, she too remains in that tradition.

I also examine other difficulties inherent in the writing of these feminists. One assumption in particular that is shared by all three writers is that pornography is produced exclusively by male writers for a male audience. However, as we see from the analysis of romantic fiction in Chapter 9, this is not the case.

In the final chapter I present my own view of what is wrong with porn. It is not primarily that pornography encourages rape or assaults on women, but that it violates the individual's – mainly the woman's – autonomy. As an object in the centrefold of *Playboy* she has given over her purpose and individuality to the whims and desires of the male consumer.

What is the solution to the problem of porn? Liberals and radical feminists disagree markedly: one proposes a free market of ideas and the other proposes outright banning. But pornography is not only about the individual's right either to buy or object to porn, as the liberals would have it, or about patriarchy, as the radical feminists would argue. Pornography is also about class, race and big business. It cannot be dealt with in isolation from these social realities, and it cannot be attributed only to male domination. Porn is a symptom of wider power relations based on gender, class and race. Only by eradicating these power relations can we hope to eliminate the ills of pornography.

The Liberal Position: Freedom of Speech

Liberals have traditionally concerned themselves with the legitimacy of state interference in individual freedoms. One freedom that has recently been in question, particularly in the USA, Canada and Britain, is the freedom of pornographers to produce, publicize and sell their materials.

The liberal position in Britain has been most clearly articulated by the Williams Report on obscenity and film censorship, produced by a committee chaired by the philosopher Bernard Williams and published in 1979.[1] My discussion of the liberal position on pornography uses the Williams Report as a touchstone, but it is by no means exclusively applicable to that document. The issues raised apply generally to the liberal position. Many of them bear, for instance, on some of the reasoning of the 1970 American Presidential Commission on Obscenity and Pornography. The view of the law in the USA, where the requirements for censorship are laid down by the First Amendment, mirrors the position defended in the Williams Report.

A significant section of the Williams Report is devoted to a set of notions to which the report gives the umbrella title 'Principles'. Included in these is a discussion of three interconnected concepts: the law, morality and freedom of expression. Here the report's fundamental concern is freedom of expression. It asks: 'what sorts of conduct may the law properly seek to suppress?' In essence, the view defended by the committee is that there is a 'general presumption' in favour of free expression; that censorship is by its nature a 'blunt and treacherous instrument'[2] and that 'weighty considerations in terms of harms' have to be brought by those who seek to curtail it.[3]

In this chapter, I explore the report's reasons for advocating freedom of expression. Along with Williams et al. I defend the notion of liberty as a fundamental value. However, I claim, and here I disagree with Williams et al., that a commitment to maximizing or equalizing liberty overall, could lead one to the view that some liberties – particularly those associated with pornography – should be curtailed.

The Williams Report and Freedom of Expression

The Williams Report begins by advancing the view, derived from J.S. Mill, that nothing should be suppressed unless it harms some-one – the 'harm' condition. Almost without exception, say the authors of the report, the submissions they received accepted this principle. They themselves fully accept it. The harm condition, they suggest, applies both to morality and the law. The main reason they give for supporting the harm condition is this:

> there is a presumption in favour of individual freedom ... incursions by governments into that freedom have to be justified; the proper sphere of government is the protection of the interests of citizens; and so what is justifiably curbed by government, therefore, is what harms the interests of some citizens.[4]

The report goes on to consider an objection to this position, voiced by Lord Devlin. Society, he argues, rests on moral consensus. Because the law protects society it can be used to preserve the moral consensus. Thus, Devlin would submit, there are circumstances under which the government may be justified in curtailing liberties, even if allowing free expression to those liberties does not harm anyone. Devlin's objection is disposed of by Hart, who urges that Devlin's view is not so much an abandonment of the harm condition as an invitation to extend it to those associated with society's moral disintegration.

The Williams Report offers its own challenge to Devlin. The latter believes that there are acts which, while not in themselves harmful, engender wide moral disapproval. If these acts are not discouraged, society will suffer. But, the Williams Report alleges, Devlin's view disallows apparently harmless acts that happen to run contrary to the majority view. The report opposes the requirement that there should be a strong moral consensus – such as, for instance, was provided by Christianity – in order for society to function well. Those who wish to curtail freedom of expression, the report warns, must bring 'weighty considerations in terms of harms'.

The lynchpin of the liberal view, freedom of expression, is justified in a quasi-Millean fashion. The classical liberal J.S. Mill, writing in the nineteenth century, had argued that people do not have infallible knowledge about themselves or anything else. They do not, therefore, know what may contribute to the development of people or society. Therefore, he urged, there should be no censorship. The only way to arrive at the truth is to allow a 'free market in ideas'. Mill believed that if all ideas were allowed expression, good ideas would multiply and bad ones would perish. Apart from the obvious difficulties with Mill's view – such as that if everyone talked at once, no truth could be arrived at, and that it is perfectly possible, as Gresham's law proclaims, that 'bad money [ideas]' may drive out good – Williams et al. none the less aver that it is basically a good thing to preserve many different points of view. Freedom of expression is therefore valuable. No further justification for freedom of expression is given in the report.

How does this apply to pornography? 'Almost all the material we are concerned with' is 'totally empty', say Williams et al.[5] Therefore, they assert, 'it will be said' that the above arguments are all very well for serious works of art or writings of intellectual content, but it is absurd to apply them to everyday, in particular pictorial, pornography. I present their response to this hypothetical objection:

> We do not claim that, directly, they do apply. But here we must stress two very fundamental points: first, that what the argument grounds is a general presumption in favour of free expression, and second, that censorship is in its nature a blunt and treacherous instrument. The value of free expression does not lie solely in its consequences, such that it turns out on the whole to be more efficient to have it rather than not. It is rather that there is a right to free expression, a presumption in favour of it, and weighty considerations in terms of harms have to be advanced by those who seek to curtail it.[6]

Apart from a brief mention of the fact that the Supreme Court of the United States has considered this issue, the Williams Report does not examine the question of whether pornography constitutes a form of expression whose suppression violates the 'presumption' in favour of freedom of speech. The Supreme Court, the committee says,

> has for a long time followed a line – though both unclearly and controversially – of arguing that the First Amendment to the United States Constitution, which says that 'Congress shall make no Law ... abridging the freedom of speech ...', does not protect hard-core pornography on the ground that such pornography is not, in a constitutional sense, 'speech': the idea being that it lacks communicative content.

But at times pornography has been deemed in the USA to be speech. American feminists campaigning on the issue, for instance, have debated the question of whether pornography constitutes 'protected speech'. Since the Williams Report's longest chapter consists of a consideration of the possible harms that might be caused by pornography, and since this section occurs in the context of a consideration of the circumstances in which curtailing freedom of expression might be justified, it would seem pertinent for the committee to have discussed the question of pornography as a form of 'expression'. However, we read that: 'happily ... this is not an issue which we are under any obligation to pursue.' One wonders why the instigators of the report were happy about this lack of obligation; one might have supposed that Bernard Williams, a philosopher, would have been quite pleased to unravel the question of what constitutes speech or expression, but he fails to do so.

Happily or not, it is a question which I believe ought to be pursued, and I shall do so in a moment. First of all, however, I would like to consider the question a little more deeply than Williams et al. are apparently able to do within the scope of a government report: why should there be this presumption in favour of defending freedom of speech and expression, and what possible grounds can there be for curtailing it? This will lead me to a more general discussion of the notion of liberty.

'No Platform to Fascists'

Many people would argue for the suppression of freedom of speech and expression in certain circumstances. The constitutions of student unions up and down the UK, for example, contain clauses refusing freedom of expression to 'fascists and racists'. And in the USA it is a principle which is constantly being tested.

A recent US case that has been much publicized concerns a Supreme Court decision that public-school officials should have the power to censor school newspapers, plays and other 'school-sponsored' expressive activities. According to the *New York Times*,

The Court held that in activities that are 'part of the school curriculum' and might seem to carry its imprimatur, officials may bar dissemination of student statements about drugs, sexual activity, pregnancy, birth control, contested political issues and other matters when doing so would serve 'any valid educational purpose'.[7]

Also reported was the attempted suppression of a book about the conception and birth of a child under a surrogate motherhood contract. The baby's father, who was awarded sole custody rights to the child, set out to block publication of the book, which was written by the mother of the baby. The judge in the case called the request to block the book 'an unconstitutional infringement of Mrs Whitehead's [the mother] right to freedom of speech'. To do so, he said, would 'violate the First Amendment and one of the fundamental premises on which the fabric of this country is based.'[8]

In the UK an event that received a good deal of attention in 1985 was the case of the National Front member Patrick Harrington, a philosophy student at North London Polytechnic whom other students sought to have excluded from classes on the ground that his professed racist views would make the atmosphere unpleasant for black students. These students submitted that his presence intimidated black students. Students demonstrated in very large numbers outside lecture halls and polytechnic buildings with the aim of denying him access. But constraints on freedom of expression have also been felt in the upper echelons of government: the former education minister Keith Joseph, for instance, has probably had his right to speak curtailed – either by legal clauses or by demonstrations preventing him from entering the places where he was due to speak – more frequently than it has been exercised.

The case of Harrington, and others less dramatic but similar in other respects, have led the British government, in its zeal to protect members of its own house, to introduce legislation requiring educational establishments to do everything possible 'to protect the freedom of expression' of visiting speakers.

What arguments are offered by those who would seek, in certain circumstances, to suppress freedom of speech? Roy Edgley, then professor of philosophy at Sussex University, defended a group of Sussex students who had prevented the American academic Samuel P. Huntingdon from giving an academic lecture in the summer of 1973. The students objected to Huntingdon's formulation of the 'forced draft urbanization' policy during the Vietnam War. A number of members of the 'liberal establishment' criticized the students and the academics who supported them as 'against free speech'.

One argument Edgley puts for his view is this: 'those who defended Huntingdon in the name of academic freedom sought to limit the freedom of those who opposed him.'[9] Thus, he asserts, one cannot unconditionally support freedom of speech. But Huntingdon was prevented forcibly from giving his lecture; we do not, therefore, have a case of conflicting freedoms to speak. Huntingdon's freedom to speak was constrained by the students' action.

Edgley, however, queries the distinction between speech and action. Richard Crossman, an ex-Cabinet minister, had said that he hoped that university vice chancellors would proclaim that 'no one can sign such a letter [a letter supporting the students' action] and remain a member of the university staff.'[10] But as Edgley points out, this constituted an attempt to suppress freedom of speech in the name of freedom of speech.

None the less, Edgley's support for his argument that one cannot unqualifiably be in favour of freedom of speech is insufficient. Those who defended Huntingdon in the name of freedom of speech sought only to allow him to speak. They did not set out to constrain his opponents. Although such restraint may have been a consequence of their actions, it was not something they 'sought' to do.

Another argument put for forcibly preventing someone from exercising their freedom to speak is that those who urge unfreedom – and it is alleged that fascists and racists are included among such people – thereby lose the right to be tolerated. Indeed, Karl Popper, himself no authoritarian, apparently endorses this view when he says that we should 'tolerate those who are tolerant.'[11] Those who would deny freedom to others, it is said, have no right to freedom themselves.

A more adroit position is that expressed by Tony Skillen. He argues that although fascists – who set out to deny freedom of expression (among other freedoms) to black people – violate consistency when they appeal in the name of freedom to have their views expressed, they do not transgress any political, or, indeed, any moral, rule. The illiberalism of a view no more justifies its suppression in the name of liberty than does the advocacy of torture merit torture in the name of humanity.[12]

When Karl Popper speaks of a 'paradox of tolerance' and contends that 'unlimited tolerance *must* lead to the disappearance of tolerance',[13] he is guilty of confusing an analytic or tautologous claim with one that is empirical. To tolerate a view that renounces freedom altogether is to accept a self-refuting proposition. Yet to accept one that harms free ways of life is not to do this at all. Indeed, Skillen argues, suppressing racist or fascist views might have precisely the effect of strengthening them. On the other hand, the advocacy of an illiberal position might strengthen freedom, perhaps because of the vacuousness of the view expressed, or because its articulation forces opponents to crystallize their position.

We can agree with Skillen and the Williams Report, then, that there is a presumption in favour of freedom of speech. Is this freedom therefore unlimited? The Williams Report, following Mill, urges that the most likely circumstances in which a restriction on freedom of expression is justified is when it 'causes harm to someone'. But Skillen goes much further. Even if an action is harmful, he says, it is not necessarily right to suppress it. Suppression, he says, is an evil in itself, *qua* restriction and frustration. Moreover suppression 'is never a mere "negation" of the act'; it involves positive institutions and practices of formulation, judgment and enforcement. "No platform", "smash the fascists" movements to suppress the expression of vicious viewpoints have helped bring about a general increase of law-and-order legislation aimed not so much at suppressing fascist groups as at imposing tighter state control of public space.'[14]

In my view Skillen does not succeed in showing that the restrictions and frustrations involved in suppressing a view constitute an evil in themselves. Restraining a child from hitting her friend may be frustrating to the child, but it does not make the action wrong. The other consideration Skillen adduces, namely that further unintended consequences may result from prohibiting the performance of an act, does not show that it is wrong to restrict the act because it is harmful; it merely points out that the advocates of restraint would have to be exceedingly careful in framing their constraints in order to avoid future unintended restrictions.

Skillen's case, therefore, is unconvincing. On the other hand, Mill's 'harm condition' is not particularly useful in deciding when to restrict freedom; as many have argued, Mill's condition does not work because no behaviour fails to harm someone. Chopping down a tree on Forestry Commission land might harm the people who regularly walk through the area; sitting at my desk in the library will harm the person who wishes to sit there, and so on. The harm condition, therefore, seems to be vacuous, and does not provide us with a means for distinguishing behaviour that ought to be restrained from action that should be unconstrained. Perhaps, however, we could distinguish degrees of harm: I am not greatly harmed, I only have a denuded aesthetic sense, by the tree being chopped down; and the person who is prevented from sitting in my seat is inconvenienced, rather than harmed. Once harmful behaviour has been so calibrated, one could argue that it is more justifiable to constrain an action that causes multiform harms or a great degree of harm than one that brings about just one type of harm or merely a little of it.

There are other ways of understanding the harm principle. It has been argued, for instance, that depriving a person of opportunities causes her harm. Even if someone's situation is not worsened, he or she may be harmed by being denied something she ought not to be prevented from having. Denying a job to a person who is hard of hearing may be harmful even though that person's situation is not worsened. Indeed, a case. like this could be said to be on a par with the infliction of pain on someone in so far as his or her life opportunities have been denied.

Perhaps we should say, then, that action should be prevented or encouraged if, as a result either of its being carried out or its not being carried out, 'severe harm' is brought about. 'Severe harm' might be characterized as physical hurt or damage to someone's sense of well-being. It might also include psychological damage.

One might, using what has come to be known as the 'doctrine of double-effect' distinguish harms which come about as the intended consequences of an action from those which are merely the foreseen but unintended consequence of some piece of behaviour. This distinction might, for instance, allow one to condemn a murder, but allow the killing of X which happened as the foreseen but unintended consequence of the attempt to save Y (who was to be the victim of X). There are, however, difficulties with this view as well.[15]

So far, then, two points have emerged: first of all, freedom of expression cannot be defended absolutely, since, as Skillen has pointed out, it is incoherent to do so. Secondly, the harm condition can be defended only if it is qualified along the lines I have proposed. I should now like to move to a different aspect of the subject and ask whether pornography constitutes a form of speech or expression.

'I do if I speak'

The philosopher J.L. Austin distinguishes 'performative' speech acts from 'constative' ones.[16] Although the distinction is not precise, it is based on the idea that some forms of speech in themselves constitute the performance of an act (other than the trivial one of uttering the words in a certain context) and not the report of its performance. Thus the utterance, 'I name this ship the Saucy Sue', is part of the christening of the ship, not a statement about the christening of a ship; 'I promise to meet you at two o'clock' is the making of a promise and not the report of the making of a promise. These 'performative' utterances are not easily characterized as being true or false. This kind of speech is not obviously cognitive; it does not clearly convey ideas that can be true or false. Yet it is speech none the less.

Champions of freedom of speech have not always distinguished its non-cognitive from its cognitive forms. Thus, those who would defend the right of the then Tory cabinet minister Enoch Powell, to have made his famous 1968 'Rivers of Blood' speech on the grounds of the defence of freedom of speech are in fact championing his right to have uttered the speech-act of warning that Britain would be overrun with black people if stricter immigration controls were not introduced. In other words, they are defending non-cognitive speech.

Some pornography clearly constitutes the expression of ideas, and these fall within the domain of 'speech' or expression, understood in the cognitive sense. The literary works *Fanny Hill*, *The Story of O* and *Justine* fall into this category. The US courts in the 1960s allowed certain publications – *Ulysses* for example – to be distributed and sold on the grounds that they were forms of 'speech seeking to communicate ideas on a subject'.[17] The judge in the case, Judge Woolsey, thought that *Ulysses* was not obscene because it was 'a sincere and serious attempt to devise a new literary method for the observation and description of mankind.'[18]

Pictorial pornography, too, could be said implicitly to express a thought, or at least to express an emotion. A picture in the centre pages of *Penthouse* or *Playboy* of a naked woman, legs splayed, eyes and mouth expressing desire, could be said to constitute an expression of the idea, 'I want you' or, 'I am ready to be devoured by you.' These pornographic depictions could be said to constitute forms of expression in the way that, for instance, a gesture made by the American President, indicating that he agrees with the British Prime Minister, may constitute the act of endorsing, and possibly reiterating what she has said. Pictorial pornography, therefore, might be said to constitute a better case of speech, in the cognitive sense, than Enoch Powell's warning. As the Williams Report assumes, therefore, pictorial porn might constitute a form of expression of ideas.

But why is it important to liberals for porn to be a form of expression? I should like to move on, now, to examine the underlying reasons for the Williams report's focus on freedom of expression.

Why Freedom of Expression?

Why do liberals focus especially on freedom of expression? One reason is that speech, it is argued, is a central human activity. The contemporary French philosopher Jacques Derrida,[19] places speech at the centre of the philosophical tradition – that dominated by *logocentrism*, the attaching of priority to the *logos* (being) – that he sets out to 'deconstruct'. Speech, in the view of the participants in the tradition, supposedly gives one direct access to thought, and thoughts, according to 'logocentric' philosophers, give one a window onto the world. Speech is therefore the form of communication least liable to error, and the most likely to get at the truth.

This is clearly an idealized picture of what speech is really like, and it is precisely this idealized picture that Derrida wishes to deconstruct. Idealized or not, however, it captures the central feature of speech that the advocates of freedom of speech believe is worth preserving – namely its cognitive aspect. A central function of speech is to express or communicate ideas. It is thereby also connected to truth. Criticizing those who silenced Huntingdon, Sir Keith Joseph wrote in a letter to *The Times* that 'some academics have lost their respect for truth.'[20] Speech, therefore, is intimately linked with rationality and its suppression involves constraining this rationality. Further, rationality is said to be an essential feature of a person's humanity. The possession of rationality has been thought, from Aristotle to Descartes and on to their twentieth-century counterparts, to be the salient feature distinguishing human beings from animals. A rational creature without the essential vehicle for expressing that rationality might be compared to a brilliant pianist without a piano.

Several defenders of freedom have appealed to this 'essence of men' as a crucial ingredient in their argument. Isaiah Berlin, for instance, whose article 'Two Concepts of Liberty' has been the most influential contemporary discussion of the topic, alleges that: 'if the essence of men is that they are autonomous beings ... then nothing is worse than to treat them as if they were not autonomous, but natural objects.'[21] Since Kant, the link between autonomy and rationality has been seen thus: people are autonomous, self-legislating beings because they are rational agents. Because they are rational agents, they are capable – and indeed, the Enlightenment view has been that they must exercise this capacity – of autonomously evaluating courses of action for themselves. Curtailing freedom, therefore, is restricting autonomy, and thus leads humanity back to its nadir, back to the 'lower' creatures from which human beings have differentiated themselves.

This is the logic underpinning the special case in defence of freedom of speech. Speech is thought to be a vital means of expressing one's rationality. But have we, speaking for the liberal, really given reasons for distinguishing speech from other forms of activity? A ballet dancer's freedom is curtailed if he is prevented from dancing by being tied to a chair, or by edict of the local council. His freedom to speak has not been removed, yet his paradigmatic means of expression has been taken away. His ballet may constitute the best way he has of expressing his thoughts. A council which stops an IRA group from marching through its town is preventing members of that group from expressing their views. Perhaps, then, the only significant difference between speech and these other forms of action is that an idea expressed through speech appears to be clearer than that put across in a ballet or in a march. Yet this is not always the case: speech may be in a language the audience does not understand; it may be incoherent, or it may be in an accent so strong that no one in the audience is able to pick out what is said. What is the point, it may be said, of preserving what is here so worthless a freedom? Think now of someone being sold into slavery. Or a person's thoughts being controlled by another. These cases constitute constraints on freedom, and we abhor constraints on freedom because they take away people's autonomy and their ability to exercise their capacities as rational agents. There do not, therefore, seem to be particularly good reasons for focusing on freedom of speech as against any other freedom. Speech, as distinct from action, contains a definite propositional content, yet this fact about speech does not appear to justify defending freedom to speak as distinct from other freedoms.

Freedom: A More General Discussion

What do we mean by 'freedom', in general? For the writer, D.D. Raphael, freedom means the absence of constraints. People are free in so far as they are not restrained from doing what they would choose to do if they knew that they could.[22] Freedom is always freedom from something, or to do something – to speak, for example. Raphael suggests that freedom is invariably the freedom to do what one has chosen to do. Moreover, he says, constraining freedom involves the deliberate action of another, and not self-imposed constraints. For instance, if I am unable to run a marathon because I am not sufficiently fit, this does not constitute a constraint on my freedom.

Raphael's view of freedom lies in a tradition of thought going back to the seventeenth-century philosopher Thomas Hobbes. Isaiah Berlin has described this conception of freedom as 'negative' freedom. One reason for defending it is that it is a simple doctrine. Another is that underlying it is a fear of totalitarianism. It is believed that any alternative conception of freedom must lead to someone other than the agent being thought to be the best judge of his or her interests and wants. Freedom of speech, then, is a form of negative freedom.

But Raphael's description of what counts as a constraint on freedom, however, is surely too restrictive. Richard Lindley makes the point by way of example:

> The story of Theseus's killing of the Minotaur ends in tragedy – the death of the hero's father, Aegeus. Theseus had agreed at the start of the voyage that, were he successful, he would hoist a white sail on his homecoming ship. If, on the other hand, he were slain, his crew would return home under the power of the original black sail. Theseus slew the Minotaur, and, after various distractions and adventures, set sail for home. But he omitted to swap the sails. His father espied the ship in the distance, and quite rationally assumed Theseus had been killed in the failed mission; for the Minotaur was a fearsome beast, and Theseus generally kept his word. According to one version of the story, despondent, he took his own life by leaping from the Acropolis. Let us suppose that you knew, it does not matter how, that Theseus was alive and successful. Benevolent concern for Aegeus would at least give you a good reason to attempt to tell him the truth about his son's mission before it was too late. But suppose you are unable to persuade him on time: for he rationally has great confidence in his son's ability, you are a complete stranger, and in any case you do not speak the same language as the king.[23]

Freedom in this case did not consist of Aegeus doing what he chose to do, for doing what he chose involved the final removal of his freedom, whereas other rational and moral considerations suggest that his choice should have been constrained in the name of his freedom. In other words, if the point of defending liberty is to enable people to act rationally and autonomously, then one could scarcely allege that these ends had been served by allowing a person, acting on what is anyway a false belief, to act in accordance with his wish to die.

There are other considerations which lead us to doubt Raphael's view that freedom consists of the ability to do what one wishes. Isaiah Berlin suggests that this condition could be met if one were simply to restrict one's wishes. Again, if the scope of what one wishes to do is very limited indeed (because of constraints on what one is able to do) then the idea of realizing one's capacities as a rational and autonomous agent is unlikely to be fulfilled. Moreover, we would not say that people were realizing their capacities as rational and autonomous agents if they were programmed to be compliant slaves, or if they were the citizens of Aldous Huxley's *Brave New World*. In these circumstances, there are no constraints on what people choose to do, but we would argue that their choices severely limit the extent to which they can be said to be autonomous.

Similar considerations apply against restricting the constraining agent, as Raphael does, to the deliberate action of another. If a child is prevented by her lack of education from exercising her capacity to read, then her freedom and autonomy are limited as greatly as they would be if someone forcibly prevented her from entering the classroom. As the contemporary philosopher Keith Graham has argued, constraints on a person's freedom might have as much to do with material factors (lack of wealth, for instance) or cultural ones (the expectation that the proper role of the Catholic or Muslim wife is to be subservient to her husband), as they have to do with forcible action. Fully fledged freedom would involve removing all such constraints.

With an eye to the difficulties in Raphael's view of freedom, Graham has suggested an alternative: '[We] define it as the absence of constraints, of whatever kind, on rational action ... associated with this ideal it will be necessary to speak of degrees of liberty, since constraints can be of varying degrees of severity as well as being of different kinds.'[24] In fact, as Graham recognizes, this conception lies in a tradition stemming from Rousseau and Kant, for whom freedom consists in obedience to rules one has rationally framed for oneself. Constraints, in this conception, are very broadly conceived, and may include, for instance, such natural phenomena as the law of gravity.

There are two problems with this wide conception of freedom, however. One is that it is too general; if we agree with its view of constraints, we can never attain absolute freedom, since no one can ever be free of the law of gravity. Surely it is important to distinguish between constraints which are physical (such as the fact that it happens to be raining today or that I happen to be living on the earth and not the moon)' from more malleable restraints (such as the absence of sufficient means to do what I would like). Constraints like the latter are restrictions that human beings can change, given rational and autonomous behaviour. Many physical constraints are not.

The other problem with Graham's formulation is that some constraints on freedom are internal to the person, and are therefore not properly described as constraints. People not only have first-order desires, but also desires about these desires; they discriminate between their wants. Some desires or goals are perceived by a person as being more significant than others. Someone may experience one set of desires as constraining another set. Suppose that I am very attached to the British Museum library. Because of my attachment, I find I cannot work at home, which is something I would like to do. Or suppose I cannot help being jealous of someone who has been promoted, and this feeling is interfering with my sense of well-being. Genuine freedom, I would suggest, would involve getting rid of desires that are preventing me from realizing other desires that I regard as being more important for my purposes. But it is inappropriate to describe my desires as constraints on my freedom.

Allowing for these two points, I would suggest a provisional formulation of freedom: freedom consists in the ability to fulfil my purposes when these purposes have been rationally and autonomously arrived at, and in the absence of (removable) constraints. Within this conception of freedom, freedom of speech and expression are simply one component part.

Pornography and Liberty: The Williams Report and the Liberal Position on Porn

As we have noted, the Williams Report concluded that: 'weighty considerations in terms of harms' have to be brought by those who wish to curtail freedom of expression. Going further than Williams et al., but along lines to which their views require them to be sympathetic, I have argued that pornographic depictions may constitute a form of expression. However, I have suggested that although freedom may constitute a fundamental right, freedom of expression is only one of its components, and cannot be picked out at the expense of other types of freedom. Again following Graham, I would argue that the notion of liberty propounded here is not simply a different concept from that defended by Williams et al. and other liberal thinkers, but one that is required by their underlying assumptions. The motivation for defending freedom of expression, as we have seen, is a belief in people's autonomy and rationality. A proper defence of these qualities requires a wider conception of freedom than that put forward by Williams.

Any commitment to the principle of liberty involves a belief that it should be maximized, other things being equal, rather than held absolutely. Edgley argued in his discussion of the Huntingdon case, that it is contradictory to be committed to the principle absolutely and under all circumstances. Richard Crossman's freedom to argue that academics who prevented Huntingdon from speaking should lose their jobs contravenes Edgley's freedom to express the view that Huntingdon should not be heard.

Complete freedom of speech according to Edgley, is self-contradictory.[25] The above is not a good example: Crossman's letter does not *prevent* Edgley from expressing his view. Yet, as Skillen points out, there *are* cases which would lead us to doubt that we can absolutely adhere to the principle of freedom of speech. Anyone who seeks to suppress someone's freedom in the name of freedom of speech is being inconsistent. Absolute adherence to the principle is impossible. Saying instead, as Williams et al. do, that there is a 'presumption' in its favour seems insufficient. My suggestion is that we set out instead to maximize liberty.

In the case of pornography, a number of freedoms must be balanced against one another. These appear to be: the freedom of the producer of pornography to go about his business; that of the designer/writer of the pictures/stories to express his ideas; the freedom of the cameraman both to make his living and to exercise his artistry; the freedom of the model to pose as she wishes; that of the consumer to buy his copy of *Penthouse*; and the freedom of the person whom pornography outrages (to use an expression from the Williams Report) not to be subjected to it. If we were to accept these as the principal freedoms, and simply tot them up, the balance might be either on the side of the pornographer or of the person 'outraged' by it. But if we add the fact of women's role in pornography, the position changes dramatically. Women (for it is invariably women) modelling for soft-core pornographic magazines present themselves as objects to be treated however the male (for again this is usually the position) consumer wishes. (The notion of 'object' is discussed more fully below.) Women, therefore, are posing to be depicted as wanting to do whatever the consumer wants to do to them. In this sense, women become the equivalent of the willing, subservient slaves of Huxley's *Brave New World* or of the Lilliputians in Swift's *Gulliver's Travels*. Though the models may have freely chosen to appear as non-rational, amenable flesh, in a crucial sense they have abrogated their freedom, and relinquished their autonomy. They appear, in Kant's phrase, as the 'means' of satisfying the man's (the consumer's) desires. Were they to be acting as fully rational beings, and in the absence of constraint, they would probably choose not to model. Constraints here include material ones – the need for a wage – and cultural ones – the premium attached to women playing this kind of role.

Williams et al. consider this line of reasoning in their report, and make two points: (a) that pornography is not a special case, since women are objectified by other cultural artefacts; and (b) the degradation of women models in pornography is not significantly different from that of the wage labourer in general. The first point is not significant. That an evil is present elsewhere is no reason for not condemning it in the case in question. This argument also applies to the report's second point. Generally speaking, wage labourers have their freedom and autonomy constrained. Their freedom not to work is restricted by their lack of wealth. None the less, there is a significant difference between the person working on the factory floor, in the coal mine, or teaching a class of children, and that of the women modelling for *Playboy* or *Men Only*. Labourers give up their autonomy only for the period of time they are working. During that time labourers sell their capacities to employers, who are free to require of the labourers that they work in accordance with the conditions of the workplace: they must extract so much coal, work so many hours, and take only a limited number of breaks. Employers cannot do anything they wish to the employees, however. They are not at liberty to beat up the employees just because they feel like it, nor are they entitled to require employees to undress, to do their shopping for them, or to play the piano.

Contrast this situation with that of the man who purchases a life-like but plastic model of a woman. Similarly, the man who buys a copy of *Penthouse* can do whatever he wishes with the representation of the centrefold model. The woman who poses for *Playboy* is allowing herself to be represented as a person whose only desire is to satisfy the wants of the magazine buyer. Although the consumer cannot enact his desires on the real woman, this woman is concurring in, and maintaining, the representation of women as images, as objects for men.

The same dynamic applies if we consider 'hard-core' porn, where more men are depicted (the distinction between 'hard-core' and 'soft-core' refers to the degree of explicitness of the sexual portrayals).[26] Here is a quote from 'Margold', a male model: 'I got into it [the porn business] for glory ... the guys want the sex – which is going to be constant – and the girls want the money.'[27] The male model depicts himself as being in a position of power over women, and as enjoying the experience of modelling; he 'want[s] people to see [him] fucking gorgeous women.'[28] The women, on the other hand, are represented by the men not as wanting something themselves, but rather as 'want[ing] men to lust after them'. This is reminiscent, as we will see in a later chapter, of the role of the heroine in a romantic fiction novel.

Hebditch and Anning point out that the 'long-term prospects' are better for male models than for female ones. The turnover is higher among women. Here is Margold on women models: 'America wants to see youth. Not under-age youth, but they want to see the 18 to 21-year-old, the baby-faced one.' Once he is in the business, the man, however, can stay there: 'Once a guy gets his dick into this business, and it functions even marginally, it stays in!'[29] In other words, although male models are objectified, and appear as 'prick' personified, they are none the less allowed to appear as real individuals, as people with personalities; women models are expected to conform to a type, an image, to an abstract conception of 'attractive womanhood'. Thus they are 'objectified' to a greater degree than men.

Since no one would rationally wish to be an object for anyone else, the perspective on freedom is now radically altered. One female model concurs with this view, but imagines that she ceases to be object merely by asserting that she is not: 'I don't mind being the subject of a sexual fantasy ... To be object ... I'm not happy with that.'[30] Maximizing overall freedom, then, might mean severely curtailing the availability of porn, if not banning it altogether. On a simple numerical argument, if no woman agreed to the representation of herself as an object, then maximizing freedom would mean restricting its availability among male consumers.

This argument begs all sorts of questions. First of all, it discounts the representational aspect of porn, a subject to which I will return in a subsequent chapter. Secondly, the argument has moved from the strictly individualistic premises of the Williams Report to collectivist ones. The person on the pages of *Penthouse* is depicted not just as an individual whose freedom may or may not be constrained, but as a woman – as a representative member of the female sex. I believe that we must take on board this collectivist view if we are to understand the ills of porn. But for now, I would like to look at the case of women models from the individualist perspective.

The kinds of harm done by pornography that Williams et al. consider are causal, behavioural consequences of its availability. They look at the possibility that it might increase rape; that it might generate violence; that it might lead to sexual arousal, masturbation and sexual intercourse (the last three of which it deems 'okay'); and that it might bring about 'deviant sexual practices'.[31] But there might be another kind of 'harm' that pornography brings about, and that is the removal of the autonomy of the individual woman modelling for *Penthouse*. She has to present herself as a means of satisfying the photographer's ends. She has to present herself, in a way that is quite unlike the requirements of other forms of wage labour, as a means of satisfying a man's desire. (This notion will be more fully explained in Chapter 9.) Intrinsic to the production of porn, therefore, is the curtailing of the individual model's autonomy.[32] And this, I would argue, is, on Williams's premises, a more undesirable state of affairs than some of the other 'harms' he considers, such as the bringing about of 'deviant' sexual practices. We could therefore argue, without recourse to the representational aspect of pornography and without regard to the non-individualistic assumption, that a case could be made for disallowing one aspect of the production and dissemination of pornography, and that is modelling.

We can make this case on the assumption that what one wants is to maximize freedom. If one is taking away one person's freedom absolutely – as happens in the case of the model – then that is likely to count for more than removing some aspect of the freedom of others. (This applies even where the model has chosen her occupation; see the discussion in Chapter 4.) But we can support the case for preventing modelling on other grounds as well. We could argue that the complete removal of autonomy should not be allowed at all, since it removes from that person, the reason for defending freedom. And, on the assumption that all individuals are equal and deserve equal consideration, we can say that no one should have their freedom removed absolutely. Thus, on two key assumptions of the liberal view and the Williams Report – the importance of individualism and autonomy – we can make a case for banning pornographic modelling altogether. As we will see when we explore two areas now being left out of the picture – the representational aspect of porn, and the individualistic premises of the report – we may arrive at very different conclusions. However, it is important to note that on the liberal assumptions of Williams et al. this conclusion makes good sense.

It might be argued that it does not follow (as I have apparently been assuming) that liberty should be maximized simply because it is desirable as an end. It doesn't follow, in other words, that one should set out to increase the overall amount of freedom. After all, maximizing freedom might mean giving one person a great deal of freedom, and another very little. Perhaps a better suggestion is that one ought to equalize it.[33] If freedom is desirable, then it is desirable for everyone and the 'presumption' in its favour is not being properly implemented if some people have none of it, and others a lot, as could be the case under the former principle. Even if one adopts this view, however, the other arguments remain.

Thus far, the argument might be represented like this: as far as pornography is concerned, freedom is often freedom for men to purchase their magazines, make their living, and read the texts of their choice. Freedom of speech, in the case of much pornography, amounts to the freedom for men to exploit women. The apparently equal distribution of freedom conceals a marked 'masculinist' bias. But, this representation of my position might continue, this reasoning parallels Marx's critique of 'bourgeois liberty' as invariably benefiting the ruling class; Marx argued that 'the practical application of the right of men to freedom is the right of man to *private property*.'[34] But I disagree with this surface reading of Marx. The exercise of freedom in capitalist societies is not invariably concerned with property, nor is the right to freedom significant only in such societies.

The radical feminist position enunciated particularly by Shulamith Firestone and Andrea Dworkin parallels the mistaken Marxist perspective. In this view, all social relations are patriarchal. 'Sex/class', the idea that the division between the sexes functions like that between classes in the Marxist sense, is the fundamental social division. The political and ideological values of the sex/class system benefit the exploiting class (that is, men) and the abolition of that system will lead to the elimination of the political values that support it. Like many Marxists, these radical feminists believe that 'liberal-democratic' values benefit one class – men – and should therefore also be eradicated.

This school of Marxist writing and radical feminism are similar in another respect: the aim of a socialist society, according to Marxists of this persuasion, is the elimination of the distinction between the private, egotistical world of 'civil society' and the world of the public citizen. 'Human' emancipation is said to be more fundamental than civil or political emancipation. But this interpretation of Marx has led some of his critics to suggest that he was advocating totalitarianism, in so far as he was supporting the elimination of the values associated with civil society. Those feminists who recommend the abolition of the family are heading in this direction. For they, too, wish to abrogate the distinction between the 'private' man or woman and the public citizen. Hence, they can also be criticized for veering in the direction of the abolition of liberal-democratic values and towards totalitarianism.

My own position, despite appearances to the contrary, is precisely the opposite. Far from advocating the eradication of liberal-democratic values, I have claimed that only a society which has removed constraints, material and otherwise, on liberty can properly be said to realize it. Since societies divided by class, race and sex necessarily entail these constraints, the abolition of these divisions is necessary for the full realization of freedom.

Conclusion

Taking the Williams Report as representative of the liberal position, I have presented the liberal case for freedom of expression. I have discussed and criticized some arguments put by those who would say that this right ought to be curtailed under certain circumstances. I have defended the view implicit in the report that pornography constitutes a form of expression but I have also argued that freedom of speech or writing – the verbal or written expression of thought – may constitute only one among several aspects of freedom. Freedom is defended because of its links with autonomy and rationality. People are only fully able to give expression to their essences as rational beings if they are free. This, I have suggested, includes removing material and cultural constraints, as well as eliminating legal and physical restrictions. In the case of pornography, there are at least two reasons, on the individualistic premises of the Williams Report, why one might seek to prevent individual women from modelling for pornographic magazines. These reasons basically have to do with the particular weight attached to the complete removal, for however brief a period of time, of autonomy.

In subsequent chapters, I will look at the two areas which were not tackled here, and which are the key to forming a conclusion about porn and freedom: the representational aspect of much porn, and the individualistic assumption of the Williams Report. But before doing that, I propose, in the next chapter, to discuss another aspect of the report – the distinction it draws between the 'public' and the 'private' domains.

2
The Liberal Position: The Public and the Private

The Williams Report concludes that the previously operational test in law for determining whether or not to legislate against pornographic works – the 'tendency to deprave and corrupt' test – is inadequate. It is designed to fit in with the harm condition, they allege; it assumes that the rationale for suppressing obscenity is the harm it causes. But, as Williams et al. recognize, pornography may be offensive not only because of its harmful effects. Pornography, they submit, involves 'making public in words, pictures or theatrical performance, the fulfilment of fantasy images of sex or violence.'[1] 'The acts represented in the images', they say, 'would be alright in private, but the same acts would be objectionable in public.'[2] Drawing heavily on this distinction between the public and the private, Williams et al. say: 'there was very broad consensus that the main objective of the law should be to protect members of the public from the nuisance of offensive material in places to which normal life happens to take them.'[3] Pornographic material, therefore, should be 'confined to those who want it' and should not offend anyone else.[4]

The report then proposes that the law be shifted onto the basis of 'public nuisance'. They recognize that some people – some women? – are not just deeply offended, but 'outraged' by pornography, and they believe that such people should not, 'in the course of normal life', be subjected to it. In addition, they think that 'children and young people' should not come into contact with it. This means that pornographic publications should not be available in 'ordinary' shops: 'positive steps should be taken to restrict the availability of a certain class of material, so that children and young people, and adults who had no interest in it, [are] less likely to come into contact with it.'[5]

We are satisfied that the restriction of pornography should be in negative terms only; that is, that it should aim only to place it behind certain obstacles, so as to protect the public at large, and young people in particular – from exposure to it. We do not advocate the setting up of pornography shops ...[6]

In other words, pornography should be made available to those who want it, and should be kept from offending those who have no wish to be subjected to it. The authors of the report recognize that the 'deep offence' felt by 'some people' is not just a matter of taste; 'reasonable people' and 'sensible people of mature taste', they submit, may be 'deeply offended' by pornography, and they should not be subjected to it.

The Private and the Emotions

Williams et al. are adamant that the law has no business interfering in what goes on in private. (They may, perhaps, simply be reporting their brief; nevertheless, this is a view defended in the report.) I would like, in this chapter, to discuss a number of meanings of the term 'private' and examine the ways in which they bear upon the reasoning of the report and on liberalism towards pornography, more generally.

It is a salient fact that, in several senses, pornographic depictions pertain to what may be called the 'private' domain. The first sense is that pornographic representations are depictions of people in various states of emotional arousal. The emotions, in one classical liberal view, are thought to be non-cognitive and non-rational, and are therefore said to be aspects of a person that lie outside the individual as a rational, autonomous agent. They lie outside the sphere of the individual as possessor of interests, and as subject to the liberal 'rights' to freedom and equality. They are, according to some, subjective and capricious, and beyond the domain of reason. They therefore belong to the domain over which the state (according to some political theorists), the law (according to others) and even morality (according to yet others) has no control.

Bernard Williams and his colleagues, who belong to the classical liberal tradition, ought on these premises to claim that the state and the law have no business interfering with pornography, since it deals in emotions, and these lie outside the legitimate sphere of state influence. According to a strict classical liberal, emotions are brute facts about us, 'raw feelings' that cannot be described as authentic or inauthentic, better or worse than one another; they are precisely the 'desires' the individual should be left alone to have.

In fact, Williams et al. bring 'the emotions' into the debate in three different ways. The emotions are the subject matter of the object of their concern, which, of course, is pornography. They are the concern of Williams et al. when they look at the effect of pornography on consumers. And thirdly, Williams and his colleagues are concerned with emotion when they examine those who dislike pornography; some of these people are said to feel 'deep offence'.

If Williams et al. were to uphold a strict liberal position they would have to say that all of these groups should be left alone to feel whatever they happen to feel. But Williams et al. are influenced by weighty bodies of opinion: the Arts Council Working Party, the committee 'which Lord Longford gathered around him', the Society of Conservative Lawyers, the Catholic Association, as well as by 'women's groups', at least some of whom must be 'reasonable people of mature taste' and many of whom argued that the law ought to intervene in these matters. Thus the report reaches a compromise solution, one which, I believe, is unsatisfactory on several counts.

First of all, the report concedes that pornography largely concerns a private matter, that is, the emotions. But instead of accepting the consequences of this, and concluding that sometimes the law has to intervene in the private sphere, as it clearly does, for instance, in the case of marriage, the report says that: 'pornography crosses the line between private and public since it makes available in the form, for instance, of a photograph, some sexual act of a private kind and makes it available for voyeuristic interest.'[7] (Perhaps one should conclude from this, as Williams et al. do not, that the public/private distinction cannot properly be drawn: does a photograph of a man crying fall within the public or the private domain? Does it only come into the public domain if it is put up for sale/'made available' in this way? Or is it sufficient that it be 'made available' to people other than the members of the family in question?) Because pornography straddles the divide, the emotions felt by those 'deeply offended' by it are legitimate objects for legislation. And yet, Williams et al. say, contradicting themselves, pornography can be disseminated in private. Why not suggest instead that pornographic depictions should be allowed to 'cross the line' between the public and the private, and that those who feel deeply offended by photos of tits and bums displayed in the shop on the corner should simply look the other way?

Williams et al. are trying to have things both ways. They allow that someone who feels 'deep offence', a classically private matter, can count as a rational, autonomous person – 'a reasonable person of mature taste' – and can have her feelings taken into consideration when legislation is being discussed. Thus they allow that the private can be public. Thus, in this one crucial respect – the division between the emotions and reason – the public/private distinction collapses. Yet the distinction is reintroduced when they say that what people do in private is a strictly private matter. So if this hypothetical 'reasonable person of mature taste' happens to spend a large part of her time – let's say through no 'rational choice' of her own – being 'deeply offended' in private then Williams can do nothing about it. Suppose this person is a woman married to someone who spanks her, in front of photos of women being spanked every time they make love. She is 'deeply offended' by this. Is she not likely to be far more 'deeply offended' than someone who shared her feelings on the subject and who glimpsed a photo in the window of a shop in Soho?

Indeed, might not the non-availability of the photo on display in Soho lead the hypothetical husband to subject his wife to more of his fantasies than she would have received had the material been on public display? This suggests that if the aim of the report is the maximization of the interests of rational people, there is no guarantee that this aim will be served by the measures it advocates.

Public and Private Persons

I have looked at one sense in which the various aspects of the pornography debate might pertain to the private realm: pornography, in various ways, deals in the emotions. But there is another sense in which the public/private divide intervenes. Classically, notions of public and private morality were linked to conceptions of public and private persons. For Aristotle, for instance, the good life was possible only through participation in the life of the *polis*, the 'final and perfect association'. Man himself was, by nature, 'an animal intended to live in a *polis*'.[8] It was in the *polis* that the highest good was attained; therefore only those people who were its citizens achieved complete good. Women, slaves and children, unlike the participants in the *polis*, did not fully realize goodness and rationality. Public persons were fully rational people who shared in the highest moral good. Private persons, by contrast, were not fully rational people. The private person achieved only the limited goodness of the 'naturally ruled', a goodness that is different in kind from that of the naturally ruling. Women shared in goodness and rationality in the limited sense appropriate to their confinement in a lesser association, the household.

Might not Aristotle's 'public persons' be comparable to Williams's 'reasonable people of mature taste' (mostly men) who participate in the morality of the *polis*/'public' space? Might not these 'people of mature taste'/'public persons' decide what to do with the 'naturally ruled'/the female objects of the pornographic magazines? Women – the objects of the magazines, the private persons – can 'share' in goodness and rationality; they can be treated as 'people of mature taste'. But they must not forget that they are 'naturally ruled'; in the private sphere, the mostly male 'people of mature taste' can do what they like with women.

Of course Williams et al.'s liberal morality is nothing like that of Aristotle. Yet a classical problem with liberal morality is the way in which it deals with the private realm. The seventeenth-century progenitors of nineteenth-century liberalism, Hobbes and Locke, self-consciously rejected the patriarchal paradigm in political thought by objecting to the idea inherent in classical thought that there was a 'Great Chain of Being' derived from the purposes or will of God. Individual human beings, in the classical picture, are neither naturally free nor naturally equal; the 'political' is neither the product of their consent, nor the means for fulfilling their needs, wants and interests. Hobbes and Locke, by contrast, insisted that the consent of naturally free and equal persons was the only legitimate basis for political authority. In order to be consistent, they ought to have extended this belief to relations between family members in the private sphere. The power of the husband ought not to have been based on natural or scriptural authority. And both do in fact insist that women as well as men are by nature free and equal individuals.[9] Yet both none the less seek to find some ground for the authority of the father and husband inside the family. They argue that there must be one authority figure in the family, and, says Hobbes, commonwealths having been 'erected by the fathers, not by the mothers of families, it is normally the case that the father is master or sovereign.'[10]

In the nineteenth century, the pre-eminent liberal J.S. Mill argued for the enfranchisement of women and for their right to participate as equals in the labour market. Yet as R.W. Krouse points out, when it came to the crunch, Mill's nerve began to fail: 'It does not follow that a woman should *actually* support herself because she should be *capable* of doing so: in the natural course of events she will *not*.'[11] Krouse puts it thus: 'Mill in the end capitulates to the traditional sexual division of labour within the family. Man is the public being, woman is the private being.'[12]

Notoriously, then, in liberal theory, the private realm has been the most likely to be exempt from the operation of liberal

principles. The private has been the most authoritarian, the
domain where people are least likely to be treated as free and
equal, autonomous beings. In their belief that they should leave
people to do what they like in private, Williams et al. are
pandering to this tradition. Of course 'leaving people alone' is
compatible with many different forms of behaviour – from physical
abuse to ideal love. But when men's private preference is to do
what they like with images of women, and when this private
preference is counterposed with a history and culture that
objectifies women and treats them as 'naturally subordinate', is it
not unlikely that relations between people in the private sphere
will be free and equal?

The 'Public' as the Institutional
The third sense of the public/private split is probably the most
politically current today. According to this version, the 'public'
domain is

> that in which institutionalized rules and practices, which define
> appropriate modes of action and interaction, prevail, including
> political, legal economic, cultural, and social institutions, such as
> legislative bodies, firms, schools, and hospitals. It also includes the
> range of actions and practices covered by the law.[13]

The private domain, by contrast, 'consists of individual actions and
inter-personal relations where these actions or relations are not
institutionally prescribed or defined, but are in principle matters
of the individual's own free choice.'[14]

Pornography indeed straddles this divide. The production, distribution, marketing, and acquisition of porn is an economic activity
and thus part of the public sphere. Its consumption may be either
public or private: men pay to look at pornographic films in public
places; on the other hand, they may read the latest copy of
Mayfair in a 'non-institutional setting'. In fact, the conclusions of
the Williams Report will affect the extent to which porn is seen as
lying on either the public or the private side of the fence, since it
prescribes 'institutionalized rules' for the production, dissemination
and consumption of porn. But is this not inconsistent? If the
report distinguishes between what are essentially public and
private spheres in its conclusion, it cannot legitimately appeal to
that distinction in determining where porn may be purchased or
consumed.

Overall, therefore, the way in which the Williams Report deals with the question of the public and private is confusing and unlikely to further its apparent aim of maximizing the interests of 'reasonable people of mature taste'. Only if the distinction between 'public' and 'private' is fundamentally rethought will this end be served.

The Public/Private Distinction: A More General Discussion

I would argue that the public/private distinction should be fundamentally rethought. Underlying the three senses of 'private' I have identified is the belief that, in the private realm, the individual should be let alone. This is the view of privacy implicit in legal conceptions; privacy is explicitly so described in several articles in the *Harvard Law Review*.[15] But this notion is not far removed from the conception of 'negative' liberty described in the last chapter. According to that notion, I am free to the degree to which no one interferes with my activity.[16] The classical liberals who advocated such liberty believed that there ought to exist a certain minimum area of personal freedom which must not be violated. If this area is interfered with, said the British liberals Locke and Mill and their French counterparts, Constant and Tocqueville, then it is impossible for men (*sic*) to pursue the various ends they find good or right. The area in question is the private realm. Classical liberals believed that we must preserve a minimum area of personal freedom. 'In the path which merely concerns himself, his [the individual's] independence is, of right, absolute. Over himself, over his own body and mind, the individual is sovereign.'[17]

The private realm, therefore, is the area of individual thought and action where others have no right to intervene (except to prevent harm to others). The family is part of this private domain. Strictly speaking, any position which includes 'the family' within the domain of the 'private' so conceived is likely to be inconsistent. For the requirement of individual freedom from constraint is likely to conflict with the liberty of the husband and father in the family to wield authority over the wife and children. I have already pointed to Mill's own inconsistency in this regard. (Plato escaped this inconsistency. In *The Republic*, Plato proposes the abolition of private property, because a love of possessions is a self-interested desire, and the aim of republic is the greatest possible happiness of the entire community.[18] Plato recognized that property could not be abolished unless the institution of the family was also eliminated. Thus women guardians were to receive the same education and training as male guardians. Plato's views were, in fact, far more at variance with the thought of his day on this subject than Mill's, yet, unlike Mill, he followed his thinking to its logical conclusion.)

But there are, as we noted in the previous chapter, even deeper difficulties in equating 'privacy' with being 'let alone'. One of Mill's arguments in defence of privacy was that only if people are 'let alone' will the truth emerge. But as Isaiah Berlin has pointed out, 'integrity, love of truth and fiery individualism grow at least as often in severely disciplined communities, among, for example, the puritan calvinists of Scotland or New England, or under military discipline, as in more tolerant or indifferent societies.'[19]

Additionally, if one accepts that a person can have conflicting desires, it cannot be the case that the truth about that person will emerge by allowing her to do what she wants. Mill's central reason for defending privacy as negative liberty does not stand up to scrutiny.

A person is not truly free if he or she is only free from external obstacles. To reiterate, freedom does not consist simply of the liberty to do as one wishes. Obstacles on freedom might have to do with material conditions such as lack of wealth. Moreover, as I pointed out earlier, 'doing what one wants' is a concept that needs unpacking. I am not truly doing what I want if I allow my desire to sit in the British Museum library to prevent me from working at home. Our identities are bound up with recognizing some goals and desires as central to the people we are, and others as peripheral. Our ability to pursue the sorts of goals classical liberals believed worthy depends on our capacity to discriminate among goals and wants. In the end, therefore, a certain interpretation of the notion of privacy and of negative freedom is incoherent; the ends the liberal believes he or she is preserving by defending negative liberty and privacy depend on rejecting these very notions. 'Negative' freedom is not sufficient for genuine liberty. Freedom or the ability to fulfil one's purposes has little to do with privacy, and much more to do with the provision of means, material and mental, for the fulfilment of one's ends.

Ultimately, the distinction between the public and private realms where 'private' is so conceived cannot be drawn. The defence of the notion of the 'private', understood in the way the liberal sees it, is ultimately incoherent, and no report on the rights and wrongs of pornography, which relies on this distinction, therefore, will be adequate.

The argument cannot rest here. Feminists have criticized attempts such as those of Plato and Filmer to eradicate the distinction between the public and the private spheres. Plato, as we have seen, advocated the 'de-privatization' of all male/female relations: the role of women in the Republic was to be, to all intents and purposes, like that of men. But, as Elshtain[20] and others have pointed out, Plato thereby slighted woman's role in reproduction and renounced her connection with Eros. Whereas men could love one another homerotically outside the 'private' sphere, little space was left for women's love for one another or for their children.

The sixteenth-century philosopher Filmer obliterated the distinction between public and private in a very different way. He argued that the role of the patriarch in the family is identical to that of the king. But feminist political theorists have criticized this view for its oversimplification of the differences between family and civil society, and its failure to acknowledge historical differences both in the relation between ruler and citizens in the state, and in the family.

Elshtain proposes a more positive approach: instead of deconstructing the family, as many feminists have done, we should present an alternative account of it, one that focuses on the construction of self, but also involves human sexuality and child development. I concur with her view. The full construction of such a position, however, lies outside the scope of this book.

Conclusion

This chapter has looked at the way in which three senses of 'public' versus 'private' bear on the reasoning of the Williams Report and liberal attitudes towards pornography. The classical liberal view to which Williams et al. are sympathetic is that the law should not interfere in private matters. In one sense of 'private' – its concern with the emotions – the law has no business in legislating against pornography. However, Williams et al., under the influence of 'weighty bodies of opinion', submit that the law must concern itself with the emotions. Thus it can intervene in the private sphere. Yet, immediately contradicting themselves, and in another sense of the term 'private', they say that it cannot. In this second sense of 'private', however, the domain of the 'private person' classically has been the area least likely to be under the sway of liberal principles. In the classical liberal tradition, patriarchal norms have infiltrated the principles governing the cooperation of 'private persons'. And these patriarchal principles, as we have seen, will be given a boost by the Williams Report's permission to pornographers to do what they like in private.

3
Individualism

I have mentioned several times, particularly in Chapter 1, that Williams, et al. and liberals more generally, rely on 'individualist' premises. In this chapter I would like to spell out what is meant by 'individualism' express some reservations about this view, and offer some alternative viewpoints. I will then return to the Williams Report and ask how these alternative viewpoints affect its conclusions.

Origins of Individualism

The word 'individualism' was coined in the 1820s,[1] but its roots lie in the eighteenth-century Enlightenment and earlier. The European Enlightenment encouraged a belief in the importance of the individual as a rational agent, able to understand and hence control the natural world. Discoveries in medicine, inventions of machinery ranging from the compound microscope to the telescope, and above all the Newtonian synthesis of the earthly and heavenly realms, encouraged an optimism that the individual was not only sovereign, but was able to control and subdue the natural world. As the German philosopher H.G. Gadamer notes,[2] the Enlightenment removed reliance on prejudice, tradition and external authority and replaced them with individual sovereignty and the powers of human reason.

The treatise regarded by cultural historians as seminal in the dissemination of Enlightenment thinking, and quoted by Diderot in his *Encyclopédie*, was Descartes' *Meditations*. This text exemplifies a certain form of individualism. In Cartesian thought the individual creates itself; as Bernard Williams argues, the Cartesian *cogito* is the expression of a performance. In saying 'I think', the subject creates itself as a self.[3] The self, for Descartes, exists only in so far as it thinks. (Perhaps Descartes is led from here to argue that the mind always thinks.) In the end Descartes doubts this 'self-authoring', as he puts it, for he suggests: 'if I were ... the author of my own being, I would doubt nothing, I would experience no desires, and finally I would lack no perfection.'[4] If he were 'the author of his own being', he would be God. Instead, he brings in God as his creator. But despite Descartes' reliance on God, he is remembered for his focus on the self and on the individual. Indeed, he is the originator of the view that the self is whole and non-fragmented, its essence transparent to itself.

Apart from Descartes, the Enlightenment thinkers Locke, Reid, Condillac, Kant, Voltaire and Rousseau focused on the reason, interests and rights of the individual conscience. Their ideas were individualist ones: a commitment to the rights of the individual, a belief in limited government, and *laissez-faire*. We can see these ideals today in the US Declaration of Independence and the UN Declaration of the Rights of Man.

Stephen Lukes points to another sort of individualism, a Romantic strain, which first appeared in Germany.[5] According to this conception, individualism embodied the Romantic ideals of individual uniqueness, originality and creativity. The two varieties of individualism, one deriving from the Enlightenment, and one from Germany, are fused in the thought of Mill.

Individualism Today

Individualism since the nineteenth century has taken two main forms. There is 'methodological individualism', according to which the individual is the basic unit of explanation; and there is 'moral individualism', where the individual is both held to be wholly responsible for his or her actions and is the unit of moral regard. The two forms of individualism are connected.

Methodological individualism is a theory about the content of social and historical explanations: any explanation of 'macro' phenomena is ultimately reducible to the behaviour, dispositions and beliefs of individuals. Society, methodological individualists would say, 'really' consists only of individuals; social events are brought about by individual people; wholes cannot do anything; understanding requires reference to individuals.

Moral individualism, by contrast, is principally a theory about the causal antecedents of decisions, projects, etc. It sees the individual as their originator. At its root is the idea of the person as a self-sufficient, whole, undivided atom that interacts only contingently with others and with the natural world. Kant espouses this type of individualism in its most extreme form. For him, the natural world plays no role at all in the motivation of a moral agent, indeed it must not. Only purely rational principles, emanating from a transcendental, purely rational self, can motivate moral behaviour. But although the Kantian version of this type of individualism is the most extreme, it only expresses in pure form the belief underlying other versions of the theory, namely that, because the individual is a rational self, the individual must be the source of all projects. (The Christian idea of the 'conscience' lies in a similar tradition: Kant's view that there is, in us, a 'self' that is capable of giving us authoritative direction that is not determined by the wants/desires we have as 'needy' beings is like the Christian idea of a 'voice in us' that tells us how to behave.) A second aspect of moral individualism is that the individual is the primary unit of moral regard. Individuals are the possessors of interests, and the bearers of rights. Locke, Hobbes and Kant are the originators of this form of individualism.

A third feature of moral-individualist thinking is delineated by a number of recent feminists.[6] Carol Gilligan suggests that a feature of moral-individualist thinking is the attachment to particular values. Moral individualists, she argues, value qualities like autonomy and duty, as distinct from other-directed values like care and concern for others. This has the following consequence:

> The definition of the self and morality in terms of individual autonomy and social responsibility – of an internalized conscience enacted by will and guided by duty or obligation – presupposes a notion of reciprocity, expressed as a 'categorical imperative' or a 'golden rule'. But the ability to put oneself in another's position, when construed in these terms, implies not only a capacity for abstraction and generalization but also a conception of moral knowledge that in the end always refers back to the self. Despite the transit to the place of the other, the self oddly seems to stay constant.[7]

Knowledge of others, in moral-individualist thinking, according to Gilligan, thus involves reproducing oneself as the other. In Kant's version, one relates to others by imagining them to be like oneself. The conception of the self involved here is, Gilligan suggests, a 'looking-glass self', a self, as G.H. Mead had thought, that is known through others' reflection. The idea behind Gilligan's thinking seems to be twofold: the 'other' - as with Lacan's idea of the self being mirrored back to itself through the 'other's' desire – functions both as the 'mirror', the means by which the self is reflected back to itself, and as another version of the self. The other is, as it were, the self reflected back.

This third feature of moral individualism is of a different order from the other two. In fact, I disagree with Gilligan's view on the connection between individualism and certain moral values. I will argue, in the next chapter, both that autonomy is a value worth defending, and that a defence of it requires that one take 'other directed' values into account. Moral individualism tends to presuppose that moral problems are decontextualized; that people are rational and impartial beings; and that relations with others are governed by equality and reciprocity.

We have, therefore, outlined three features of moral individualism: (i) the individual is the causal antecedent of decisions/projects, etc.; (ii) the individual is the primary unit of moral regard; (iii) the moral individualist attaches importance to certain values – such as autonomy – as opposed to 'other-directed' values.

What C.B. Macpherson[8] calls 'possessive individualism' – the theory held more or less steadfastly by Hobbes, Harrington and Locke – is a subspecies of moral individualism. According to Hobbes, in Macpherson's view:

1. What makes an individual human is freedom from dependence on the wills of others.
2. Freedom from dependence on others means freedom from any relations with others except those relations which the individual enters voluntarily with a view to his or her own interest.
3. Individuals are essentially the proprietors of their own persons and capacities, for which they owe nothing to society.
4. Although individuals cannot alienate the whole of their property in their own persons, they may alienate their capacity to labour.
5. Human society consists of a series of market relations.
6. Since freedom from the wills of others is what makes an individual human, each individual's freedom can rightfully be limited only by such obligations and rules as are necessary to secure the same freedom for others.
7. Political society is a human contrivance for the protection of the individual's property in his or her person and goods, and (therefore) for the maintenance of orderly relations of exchange between individuals regarded as proprietors of themselves.

The first, second, third and sixth points are implicit in the description I have so far given of moral individualism. The fourth, fifth and seventh are Macpherson's additions, derived from the thought of the seventeenth-century natural rights theorists, which he argues are inherent in individualist thinking. It is logically possible, however, to be a moral individualist without being an apologist, in Macpherson's sense, for capitalism.

How do people argue against individualism? Methodological holists argue that the reduction to individuals required by methodological individualism cannot always be carried out (the precept is impossible to put into practice) and argue at other times that if it is imposed on the science it will distort it. Thus, holists would say, it is not true that explanations in terms of social wholes – families, economic forces, classes – are reducible to explanations in terms of individuals. The two types of explanation are quite distinct. Methodological individualism is neither a true nor a useful description of what goes on in the sciences. I believe that one can make the same type of claim about 'moral' individualism.

For Kant, as we saw, individualism ironically involves stripping the person of all qualities that, in fact, make for individuality. John Rawls[9] – the modern Kant – shares this view. Rational moral choice, for Rawls, under the condition that I am one of a group of free and equal persons, each of whom has an idea of 'the good life', must not involve my personal idea of it, nor must I make reference in making my choices to any individuating information about myself, such as my age, sex, race, generation, religion, class or abilities. Rawls' 'veil of ignorance' rules out considering these qualities. Just as atomic theory strips away the individuating features of particular substances, and reduces them to the respects in which they are all alike, so too does moral-individualist theory set out to make people alike. Obviously the rationale behind Rawls' and other ethical theorists' views is that they want to consider only morally significant facts, and it is therefore supposed to be a virtue of their theories that, despite our inequalities and differences, as moral beings, as the possessors of interests, we are alike and equal. Indeed, as rational beings we are alike and equal.

In reality it is not always true that certain facts about people, facts that contribute to individuating them, are morally irrelevant. The action of a white man beating up a black man in a pub, where the latter's colour contributed to the white man's anger, is not just wrong because beating people up is in general wrong. It is wrong because the person's race was in question, and because black people have been treated badly relative to whites. It was surely a recognition that the facts of inequality are not morally irrelevant, that led the seventeenth-century natural rights theorists to argue that, in addition to the natural rights to life and liberty, there is a right to property. Property is not intuitively, as life and liberty are, something to which one might suppose oneself to have a natural right. It is plausible to suppose that people are equal in respect of their possession of life and liberty, but it is very unlikely that they will ever be equal in the possession of property. Natural rights theorists might as well have argued (although it may be significant that they did not) that there is a natural right to being a man (as opposed to a woman) and perhaps to being white. (Although there is, of course, the difference that it is theoretically possible to distribute property equally, but not 'maleness' or 'whiteness'.) This is, in effect, a counter to a 'moral-neutralist' perspective. Moral neutralism is basically the view that 'agent-relative' concerns are irrelevant when considering moral goals. In the next chapter, I will consider some pros and cons of moral neutralism.

The individualist might respond here by saying that he is merely claiming that I am solely responsible for what I do. This is surely the case. The white man is responsible for his action. I do not believe that this is all that the individualist is saying. But even this view is open to question. Its questioning will lead me to one of the alternative theories to moral individualism, and this is 'moral' holism or 'moral' collectivism. But first I'd like to expand on some of these arguments against moral individualism.

At the root of moral individualist thinking is the Lockean ideal of the person as a given atom, possessing certain pre-social rights to life, liberty and property. Locke's atomic self is Descartes' ego: the self that exists because it thinks; the self whose existence is given to it without reference to any other (except God).

Now, there is a tradition of thought coming down through Fichte, Schelling and Hegel that challenges this Cartesian conception. According to the latter, self-consciousness consists of a relation where the subject looks at itself, and grasps its identity with itself. But, Fichte argues, in the very activity of reflection, the self is presupposed; if the subject of the act of reflection were not the self, then the 'object-self' of which it comes to have knowledge could not be identical with the self. Additionally, unless the subject self is already acquainted with itself it cannot recognize itself in the object. Fichte and Schelling develop their own anti-Cartesian theories. Hegel's response to Descartes is to argue that it is only in relation to an 'other' that is distinct from the self – indeed, an 'other' that is itself self-conscious – that the self can gain awareness of itself as a self. I shall have more to say on this subject in Chapters 8 and 10. But for now suffice it to say that the self is only formed, in the Hegelian view, in a 'social' context.

Another way of putting this might be to say that society is built into the individual; that individuality is formed, as many sociologists have argued, out of social elements. The 'generalized other' of liberal individualist theory is an ontological impossibility, a logical lunacy. It cannot be individuated. The 'other', in the end, disappears.

The liberal individualist may respond, at this juncture, that moral individualism only requires an *assumption* that the subject is a detached atom; not that he or she is so in fact. Psychologically or sociologically, so the objection may run, I am no doubt formed in conjunction with my fellows, but this need not touch the liberal assumption.

But can social concepts ever properly come into being on the strict liberal individualist premise? Hegel and Rousseau argued that one cannot deduce social concepts from individual wills; for them, social reciprocity is required if social concepts are to gain a footing. Property and contract, they would argue, the concepts by means of which the Lockean individual moves from the state of nature into society, themselves acquire their meaning only in a social context. Thus Locke cannot use the defence of property (including life and liberty) to explain why the atomic individual moves out of the state of nature into a society based on consent; the very meaning of these concepts presupposes that social setting.

Even if individualists are not convinced by this objection, there is a further difficulty with liberal individualist thinking. The atomic self of liberal individualist theory – the Kantian or Rawlesean self – is put beyond the reach of experience. No project could ever call into question the person that I am; I am independent of the values that I have. But this rules out the possession of a public life in which people's very identities could be at stake. It removes the possibility that common purposes and ends could bring about different self-understandings. It eliminates the influence of the community on the formation of the subject. These are serious limitations on individualist theory; below we will see what the alternatives to individualism have to offer.

Moral Collectivism

Moral collectivists hold an ontological position that the world contains not only individuals but collectives. They further believe that collectives, as distinct from individuals, can take responsibility for action. Keith Graham, who puts this view in *The Battle of*

Democracy, gives the example of a jury:

> Jane Smith holds and expresses views as to whether the prisoner is
> guilty. But this has no significance except in so far as she does so in
> the appropriate circumstances as a member of the jury. We can
> describe her various activities in purely individual terms, and the
> actions of the jury are themselves reducible without remainder
> into similar activities undertaken by other such individuals. But it is
> only by a backward loop which brings in again the collective term
> 'jury' that the peculiar relevance of these activities is revealed.[10]

Graham goes on to argue that there are circumstances in which
we must argue that it is the collective, and not the individuals it
composes, that is morally responsible for the action taken. The
example he gives is a university senate, made up of members X, Y
and Z, that resolves to close one of the university departments. He
argues that although X, Y and Z can be held individually to account
for being members of the senate in the first place, and for taking
part in the decision-making process, it is the senate as a collective
entity, and not X, Y or Z, that is causally responsible and hence can
be held morally to account for the action.

In the two cases Graham considers, the collective is a group of
people voluntarily brought together, and sharing certain interests,
to perform a certain function. But, he suggests, not all groups will
be like this: not everyone will engage in corporate action, nor will
the collective necessarily contain members who think of
themselves as an interest group. He suggests that it will often be
appropriate, following the line of thought suggested in the jury
example, to attribute responsibility to a person not *qua* individual,
but *qua* member of a particular collective. Thus – to extrapolate
from his argument – it may be appropriate, in certain circumstances
to blame 'the white man' and not John Smith for an action taken
against a black person.

I would argue that men can be treated as a group in Graham's
sense. The group 'men' is unlike the group 'jury' in that the latter
has a clearly defined membership, and a collective identity. It
makes no sense to refer, as we can to a jury, to 'a men'. Men are not
an interest group. Yet, I would argue, we can ascribe blame and
attribute responsibility to men as a group.

There is plenty of evidence that throughout history women have
been exploited. There have been several attempts to explain what
this phenomenon means (see, for instance, Janet Radcliffe
Richards's: *The Sceptical Feminist*). A provisional definition of this

exploitation might be the systematic and unjust treatment of women as inferior to men. It is not inappropriate to claim that men, as a group, are responsible for this state of affairs. Of course there are many individual men who have not exploited women; there may be several or many members of a jury who disagree with the decisions taken by the collective body. But the individuals who disagree can still be held responsible for the actions of the collective.

There is another 'non-individualist' perspective. Carol Gilligan's critique of moral individualism suggests that its 'atomistic' perspective omits the possibility of 'other-directed' behaviour. If one thinks in terms of the values implicit in it – autonomy, duty, obligation – 'other-directed' behaviour becomes placing oneself in the position of the other, but where the self is unchanged. If, however, one's capacity to know others is construed as, (in Gilligan's words) 'a joining of stories', or, to use an expression from H. G. Gadamer,[11] a 'fusion of horizons', then knowing others might generate new knowledge and the self might be changed in the process. An 'other-directed' morality would emphasize qualities like attachment, care and engagement, qualities that tend to be left out of the individualist account. The self is the opposite of that posed by the individualist perspective; it is intrinsically social because its core is constructed, according to contemporary object-relations psychoanalysts, relationally.

The self is thus internally, through the internalization of other figures, as well as externally, related to others. In this perspective, the appropriate alternative to the individualistic view would be a 'relational' one: individuals are members of collectives; they are also related to other people, and not isolated atoms. Some feminists have argued that the relational self generates a morality of sympathy, care and concern, a morality that has affinity with Aristotle's notion of virtue, and one that is *prior* to the morality of social-contract theory. One can begin to uncover it, they argue, by looking, as an example, at the special relationship of care between mother and child.

How would the relational self deal with the question of moral responsibility? Earlier I argued, following Graham, that it may sometimes be the individual *qua* member of a collective, and not the individual on his or her own, who can be held responsible for an action. Here we could say that it may be someone other than that individual – an 'other' who is internally related to the self – who is responsible. We are familiar with the idea of blaming the mother, or sometimes the father, for a child's behaviour. We do not mean that the mother is literally the causal agent of the action, but we do mean that the child is carrying out the action because it has introjected that part of the mother's values. This idea could be extended to other cases. For instance, a general in an army could be said to be the one who is really responsible for the soldier's action in killing an enemy soldier, although, again, he is not the causal agent of the action.

I should like to support this non-individualist perspective by offering one further argument against moral individualism. Rawls proposes the following two principles of justice:

> First: each person is to have an equal right to the most extensive basic liberty compatible with equal liberty for others. Second: social and economic inequalities are to be arranged so that they are both (a) reasonably expected to be to everyone's advantage, and (b) attached to positions and offices open to all.[12]

The 'basic liberties' for Rawls are 'political liberty' together with freedom of speech and assembly, liberty of conscience, freedom of thought and freedom of the person along with the right to hold personal property.[13] Rawls argues that equal liberties entail 'self-respect': 'a person's sense of his own value, his secure conviction that his conception of his good, his plan of life, is worth carrying out.'[14]

However, Rawls' individualism counts against his commitment to liberty. For he cannot guarantee, as his position requires him to, that people's self respect is not related to their relative positions in the distribution of power, income, etc. – in other words, partly to their membership of various collectives. Indeed, their membership of these collectives may undermine the equality of liberties: inequalities of income, wealth and power may affect the degree to which different groups can make use of their 'formal' liberties. Thus Rawls' individualism' cuts across his commitment to the liberal value of liberty. Not only do liberty and individualism not necessarily go together, but they may be incompatible values.

A non-individualist perspective, it might be said, adopts an unrealistic view of people as intrinsically selfless and other-regarding. Additionally, it eliminates any genuine differentation between people as well as individual autonomy. Therefore, some form of individualism must be correct. But as we will see in the next chapter, the 'collectivist' perspective is not only not incompatible with individual autonomy, but a presumption in favour of autonomy actually requires this viewpoint. For now I would only concede that some degree of self-interest is both realistic and desirable so long as it is not directed towards destructive ends. A self-interested pursuit of money at the expense of others is undesirable; however, a self-interested devotion to a cooperative project rebuilding a village in India may, despite Kant, be highly desirable.

I have now offered some arguments against moral individualism, and two alternative viewpoints have been presented: moral 'collectivism' and moral 'relationism'. In the final part of this chapter, I will return to the Williams Report, and ask the question: how do the arguments of this chapter affect our reading of it?

The Liberal Position on Pornography and Collectivism/ Relationism

The model who poses for *Penthouse*, *Playboy* or *Men Only* is invariably a woman. The photographer, the owner of the magazine, and the consumer are usually men. The owner of the magazine is probably rich. Their membership of these groups is morally relevant in deciding our attitude towards porn.

When I considered the question of maximizing or equalizing freedom, I viewed people as individuals with conflicting interests and equal rights. But the individualist perspective hides some of the ills of porn. The position is radically altered once we add that these people are not just individuals, but members of various groups and essentially inter-connected with others. The photographer's right to take a picture of a naked woman is not an equivalent right to that of the person 'deeply offended' by porn not to be so affected. They cannot be treated just as two individuals with rights, each of which demands fulfilment. The photographer is probably a man, a member of a group that has throughout history exploited women.

One form that this exploitation has taken is the turning of woman into an image. The contemporary French philosopher Luce Irigaray, throughout her writings and particularly in her work *Speculum of the Other Woman*,[15] connects the use of visual imagery with masculinity. Female nature has been characterized in the western philosophical tradition, Irigaray suggests, by lack, and a lack of something visible. By virtue of her lack, woman becomes, in the western philosophical tradition, 'other': she is complementary to what is normal, superior, given. When the Freudian or Lacanian little girl, Irigaray posits, looks in the mirror, what she sees, since the focus of her looking is supposed to be the penis, is nothing.

Woman is what masculinity is not: she becomes associated with qualities that the masculine man either does not possess, or that he seeks to transcend: the womb, the earth, matter, receptacle or, in the Freudian case, nothing. Sometimes, as in the thought of Plotinus, from whom Irigaray quotes, the woman becomes the proverbial Lacanian mirror.

> [matter] pretends to be great and it is little, to be more and it is less, and the existence with which it masks itself is no Existence, but a passing trick making trickery of all that seems to be present in it, phantasma within a phantasm; it is like a mirror showing things as in itself when really they are elsewhere ...[17]

Woman is matter, and matter is like a mirror. Woman becomes herself the medium in which the little boy sees himself reflected back. Irigaray argues in her essay on Freud that he was dominated by the 'logic of the same' because he really recognizes only one set of qualities – the masculine ones – and the feminine is seen as what is not masculine. Throughout the tradition, the positively valued male qualities – intellect and reason – have been associated with vision. Either the process of knowledge is discussed in visual terms, or visual metaphors are used to express these positively valued masculine qualities.

In her discussion of Descartes, Irigaray extends further the idea that visual imagery is connected with masculinity. Descartes looks inside himself and sees that he thinks and therefore that he exists as a thinking thing. Thus, she says: 'the subject's existence and reflection works like the backing of a mirror that has been introjected, "incorporated", and is thus beyond perception.' The subject looks in at himself in the mirror he has introjected, and sees himself reflected back. But, she says,

> What if illusion were constitutive of thinking? What if therefore the crucial thing to do were rather, or especially, to conclude that the other exists – and the self in the other – from the fact of thinking? What if I thought only after the other has been inserted, introjected, into me? Either as thought or as a mirror in which I reflect and am, reflected.[17]

Several other writers have argued that the 'ideal' spectator is assumed to be male, and that the image of the woman is designed to flatter him. Many European painters who painted female nudes (Rubens and Tintoretto, for example) assumed a male viewer. By contrast, on the rare occasions when women have portrayed male nudes, or publicly taken pleasure in the male body, they have often been criticized. One of D.H. Lawrence's gamekeepers complains that his ex-wife had looked at him as if he were a Greek statue. And, as one feminist writer points out, 'when in England there was a temporary and joking fashion for male strippers entertaining women in pubs, one judge, trying a proprietor for keeping a disorderly house, treated the case as if it marked the end of civilisation as we know it.'[18] Prudishness, she reminds us, was one of the defining traits of bourgeois femininity.

Thus men as a group have taken pleasure in turning women into images; in representing the female body as desirable to them. Male sexuality today, which is a lot more visual than women's, reflects this. The turning of women into images is part of men's exploitation of women. Turning an 'other' into an object need not be exploiting them. Calling a woman a 'cunt' or a 'piece of ass' is not necessarily exploitative. But if it occurs in a situation in which women are generally treated in this way, it is unmistakably exploitative. So, too, is treating a woman as a body, and not as a person. Men as a group can be held responsible for the action of the individual photographer.

The individual who models for a pornographic magazine does so as a woman. It is not the person Samantha the reader looks at (although *Penthouse*, *Playboy* and *The Sun* like to play on the individuality of the women on its centre pages), but a picture of a naked woman. Samantha acts as a representative woman. Yet women as a group are not responsible for this action. Using the argument that we all stand in internal and external relations to others, we can say that it is the men whose values the model has internalized who are responsible. Instead of speaking of the right of the model to pose as she wishes, we should refer to men's responsibility for the belief, which the model has internalized, that there is nothing wrong with turning her into a desirable image.

It is wrong to exploit women. If porn contributes to this exploitation it should be banned. However, there are competing considerations that may prevent us from coming so readily to this conclusion. The model is not just a woman; she may also be rich and a white person. The photographer is not merely a man. In rare cases, he may be a single parent, black and poor. We have to balance out the rights and responsibilities of rich white people towards poor black people, and non-parents towards parents, against those of women and men. Perhaps the model does not much need the money, whereas the photographer desperately does. Perhaps he has looked hard for other work and has been unable to find it.

Finally, however, overriding importance must be attached to the membership of particular genders rather than of other groups. It is most unlikely that all pornographic photographers are single parents, black and poor. Many models, on the other hand, are black and not rich. In the case of porn, the group whose rights should prevail is women, because most models are women and many pornographers are men.

Feminism and the Liberal Position on Porn

The liberal position on porn, as represented by the Williams Report and the US Constitution, relies on moral individualism. In the liberal view, people are self-sufficient, whole atoms that intersect only contingently with others. The only unit of moral regard and blame, for the liberal, is the self. This perspective, I have argued, hides some of the ills of porn. In order to see more clearly what is wrong with porn, we need to adopt the collectivist viewpoint. Feminists who enter the liberal individualist debate compromise themselves. Feminists in the USA, for instance, have argued that pornography ought not to be protected under the First Amendment because it constitutes a 'clear and present danger'. Rosemary Tong[19] distinguishes three stances feminists have taken in arguing for the harmfulness of what she calls 'thematic' pornography. Thematic porn represents sexual exchanges devoid or nearly devoid of mutual or self-respect; it shows sexual exchanges which are degrading in that the desires and experiences of at least one participant are not regarded by the other participant(s) as having a validity and a subjective importance equal to his/her own. Tong explains the three feminist positions: '(1) Although such thematic material may not be harmful *per se*, it causes people to engage in harmful behaviour; (2) Thematic material does not have to be harmful in order to be constitutionally censorable; and (3) Thematic material is harmful.'

These feminists, in other words, are entering the debate on precisely the liberal individualist terms of Williams et al.: they refer to 'people' independently of their gender, and they talk of 'harmful' consequences. Yet another feminist argument that repeats the reasoning of the Williams Report is this: even if porn is not harmful, pornography is offensive to most women and, to the extent that it is publicly flaunted, action should be taken against it. We have already pointed to the weakness of the harm condition and have criticized the report's insistence that it is only the 'public flaunting' of pornography that is objectionable. Feminists, in entering the debate on these terms, are necessarily compromising themselves, because its frame of reference does not properly allow them to express what is wrong with porn.

Only the concept of 'group libel' allows one to move away from the individualistic premises of liberal thinking. If all members of a class of people can be libelled, then the collectivist assumptions can be brought out. Some American feminists have moved in this direction. Pornography could be libellous towards women as a group. But, as Kittay points out,

> there are separate problems here: for a statement to be libellous, it must be a statement of fact that can be proven to be false. The libellous content of much pornography does not easily lend itself to such proof, particularly when much of it (a) is so widely assumed to be true and (b) is also believed to be the sort of thing that a woman will not easily admit to. Take, for example, the implicit or explicit claim that women want to be raped as a characteristic but libellous claim found in much pornography. Within our culture, men and women alike think that a woman saying 'no' does not justify a belief that she meant 'no', and girls are still taught that they ought not to be open and honest about their sexual feelings. [20]

Underlying Kittay's argument is the view that what is morally wrong with porn is what is morally wrong with patriarchal society in general; one will not root out the latter by attempting, by legal means, to get rid of the former. Any legal strategy, as I will argue later, is therefore, likely to be problematic, because one cannot eliminate patriarchy by legal means.

I have considered one sort of argument that leads to the conclusion that porn should be banned. Another argument leads in the same direction. One could argue that there is a 'presumption' in favour of love, care and concern for others, and that pornography consistently violates this. It encourages selfishness (in the satisfaction of desires), a lack of interest in the other's point of view, and the treating of the 'other' – the fantasy object – not as someone whose stance can shape, inform or alter one's own, but as a person onto whom one's - invariably the man's – fantasies are projected. Porn involves an exclusively 'individualist', as opposed to an 'other-directed', view of the self. Once more, then, one is led to the conclusion that porn should be banned.

Conclusion

In this chapter I have outlined two forms of individualism, methodological and moral. I have expressed various reservations about individualism, and presented 'collectivism' and 'relationism' as alternatives. Finally, I have argued, that the collectivist arguments lead, contrary to Williams, to the conclusion that porn should be banned. In fact, as my argument progresses, I will modify this conclusion, since in the end it does not serve any useful purpose. It is, however, the logical outcome of the argument thus far.

4
Autonomy

In the previous chapter, I criticized one aspect of the liberal tradition, namely, its commitment to 'moral individualism'. Some liberal values, however, are significant and worthy in their own right. I have already defended liberty. Another such value – a concept that is integral to the liberal and individualist tradition – is autonomy. This notion, like liberty, is important not just for liberals: indeed, it is a concept that may be of use in developing an anti-sexist, anti-racist and anti-class politics.

In this chapter I shall argue that there is not a necessary connection between autonomy and individualism. I will go further, and suggest that belief in autonomy requires one to take seriously the values of a 'relationist' perspective.

Autonomy and Individualism

Nancy Chodorow[1] suggests that the perspective of object-relations psychoanalysis, which questions the individualistic viewpoint, also poses a radical challenge to 'wholeness and autonomy'. A self that is intrinsically social and includes 'aspects of the other' – in other words, a 'relational' self – subverts autonomy as a value. Carol Gilligan connects the attaching of importance to the values of autonomy, duty and obligation, to the individualist, separate and bounded, self. Her argument is that the individualist conception of the self 'predisposes' one morally towards an 'internalized conscience' enacted by the will, and 'guided by duty and obligation'. Even the notion of 'putting oneself in the other's shoes', she argues, does not get away from the focus on the self as an isolated atom. Autonomy is supposed to be a value that is internally connected with the individualist, isolated, discrete, atomic self.[2]

One can understand why this connection should be made. Kant, for instance, usually thought to be the prime defender of autonomy, believes that the moral self is not only discrete and atomic, but is severed altogether from the natural world. It becomes a transcendental ego, a non-bodily thing. Kant regards action motivated by care and concern as completely distinct from morality, as allowing the dictates of the emotional, natural, non-rational self to hold sway over the properly moral self – the purely rational ego. Allowing ourselves to be motivated by care and concern, for Kant, would be tantamount to giving precedence to those human features which are shared with other animals: emotions, appetites and drives. In Kant's view, only behaviour which is untainted by the emotions is properly rational and autonomous. Not only must it have nothing to do with inclination, but properly autonomous action must apply to all people, and not just to oneself. It must not concern only one person, rather one must: 'Act only on that maxim through which [you] can at the same time will that it should become a universal law.'[3] A person who acts on universal principles is truly autonomous; his or her actions are 'other-directed' only in the sense that all the qualities that differentiate the self from others have been removed. Behaviour, therefore, is 'other-directed' in so far as one becomes 'like' the other. As we have seen, this is very different from the 'other-directed' action of the 'relational' perspective, where the individual attempts not to be like the other by abstracting away all individuating features of oneself, but rather to understand the other, to 'fuse' his or her horizon with the other's.

One can understand why autonomy and individualism are seen as linked. Actions that are autonomous are motivated solely by principles that derive from oneself. An individual person is the source of value. The focus, for the autonomous self, is the self. Others somehow seem to be left out of the picture.

But this perspective on autonomy is misleading. Contrary to its assumption, a presumption in favour of autonomy can be defended only if one's behaviour is other-directed. I'll argue this by presenting, and defending, a notion of autonomy.

Autonomy and 'Caring': 'Other-directed' Behaviour

According to Kant, there are two strands to autonomy. First of all, autonomy is, as we have seen, pure rationality. To be autonomous, a person has to be a purely rational self unmoved by particular considerations. The grocer who gives all her vegetables away because she is inclined to do so is not acting autonomously, and therefore her action, for Kant, does not have moral worth.

There are well known difficulties with this feature of Kant's perspective. For one, it makes it impossible to account for wrong-doing. Wrong-doing is presumably action motivated by a self-centred inclination. If we are only morally responsible for behaviour that is motivated by purely rational considerations, then we are not morally responsible for wrong-doing. On the other hand, if one person chose to be wicked on purely rational grounds, then, in the Kantian view, everyone ought to do the same. Either way, the conclusion is absurd.

Furthermore, it is impossible to see how behaviour can be motivated solely by purely rational principles. People are natural beings and their behaviour is causally motivated by events in the natural world. It is ridiculous to suppose that a transcendental, purely rational self can influence behaviour in the natural world. A purely rational self could be responsible only for further 'purely rational' matters, and not for any other behaviour. In any event, even 'purely rational motivation' must be caused by natural desire or inclination.

The second strand of Kant's theory can more easily be defended. The second part of his theory instructs us to 'Treat humanity, whether in your own person, or in that of any other, never simply as a means, but always, at the same time, as an *end*.'

Kant himself thought that the first and second points were linked. One is treating a person as a means, his argument runs, if one fails to regard them as a purely rational being, as a person who acts from rational considerations alone. In fact the two are not necessarily connected. We can reject his version of the self as a purely rational self while accepting a version of his second assumption.

People are not purely rational selves in the Kantian sense. They also have inclinations and desires. These inclinations and desires, as Hume recognizes, partly determine the goals they pursue. Hume argues against Kant that motivation by reason alone is impossible. But he goes too far in the opposite direction, arguing that only preferences or desires determine the ultimate ends we pursue. According to him, we choose among different ends – whether to be Muslim or Christian, for instance – according solely to the strength of our desire for either religion. But surely this is not right. I can rationally decide which of the two to opt for.

Human beings deliberate about their wants and beliefs. A non-human (non-rational) animal acts on the basis of whatever inclination is strongest at any given time, but people are able to postpone (or give up altogether) immediate gratification in the light of the likely consequences of satisfying that desire, or of conflict between it and some other wish. I may forgo that desperately 'needed' cigarette after listening to a speaker on the dangers of smoking.

The philosopher Harry Frankfurt argues that rational beings have different levels of desire. For instance, I may desperately want a cigarette, but I may also want not to get cancer. And I may believe that there is a statistical link between smoking and lung cancer. Frankfurt uses the notion of different levels of desire to explain freedom of will: 'to identify an agent's will is either to identify the desire (or desires) by which he is motivated in some action he performs, or to identify the desire (or desires) by which he will or would be motivated when or if he acts.'4 Not all of my desires – even the desire to smoke – will be put into practice. According to Frankfurt, 'the will' is not the total sum of a person's wants and desires, but only those wants and desires that are expressed in action.

An important part of Frankfurt's case is what he calls 'second-order volitions'. These are not just desires, but desires about desires. Second-order desires are wants arrived at after deliberation about first-order desires: I will quell my desire to smoke because I do not want to get cancer. A person has freedom of the will, Frankfurt says, if he or she is able to make these second-order desires the 'effective' ones. Freedom of the will has to do with being able to make one's will as one wants it to be. We can therefore say, following Frankfurt, that being able to make one's will as one wants it to be is a necessary condition for treating oneself, or another, as an end and not as a means.

Again we find difficulties. As in the case of Aegeus in Chapter 1, there may be people whom we would not describe as 'treating themselves as ends' because they are not fully able to evaluate their wants. Aegeus lacked the information which would have redefined his wants. Another example would be someone who did not have the second-order desire not to smoke because they had simply decided to ignore the information on smoking and lung cancer. This illustrates that the above condition is necessary, but not sufficient, for 'treating X as an end'. It illustrates, indeed, why Kant imposed the other condition on autonomy. For what is missing in these cases is the idea of the self acting as a rational agent on the basis of information made available to it by other rational agents.

We do not need to return to Kant's rational self in order to modify the above condition. We could add to it that the self is treating itself as an end if it is able to make its will as it wants it to be, when it has had all relevant information put to it, and when it is acting out of a disposition to seek the best way of behaving. This is a modified version of Mill's idea that since people's knowledge is limited they ought actively to seek out the truth. Treating someone as an end involves that person acting on the basis of their wants when those wants have been arrived at by the person acting rationally, and in the presence of relevant information.

What would count as 'relevant information'? At the very least, it is information which is such that, had the agent had it, and had she deliberated, she would have had different desires from the ones she originally had. We must tread carefully, however. For the condition might easily become far too broad. If I came to be in possession of information about possible jobs in the USA, I might choose to spend the day applying for them instead of choosing to sit writing this essay; if Jones had been in possession of information telling him which horse would win the Derby, he would have wanted to bet on that horse instead of wanting to go fishing. The information has to be information about the want in question, that might have led the agent, had she had it, not to have wanted what she once wanted. The suggestion is that people should be in possession of as much information as possible: obviously they cannot always know everything they might know about the want; Aegeus clearly did not. Someone who does not know of the link between smoking and cancer does not.

But it is not always lack of information that prevents someone from acting autonomously. Other constraints may prevent someone from choosing to do what, in the absence of those constraints, they would opt to do. For instance, a coalminer may not want, after rational deliberation, to work down the mine, but will recognize that she must if she is to survive. Drawing on the view of freedom defended in the first chapter, we can say that a person is not fully autonomous unless all constraints that are potentially removable by people acting rationally – including those imposed by lack of means and by culture – are removed. A provisional definition of what it is to treat X fully as an end is: X is treated as an end if X acts on the basis of her own wants, wants that have been rationally arrived at, when all removable constraints on her arriving at them have been eliminated.

Autonomy is not an all-or-nothing matter. Rather, it comes in degrees. The definition applies to full autonomy, but, I will argue, some autonomy is better than none.

Autonomy and Care

From this line of reasoning we can see that the self is not an isolated, individualistic, discrete unit. In order for X to be autonomous, she needs to be provided with the relevant information. If Y is interested in X's autonomy, and if Y is able to provide information affecting it, then Y is obliged to provide that information – in the interest of X's autonomy. The person in possession of the true facts must tell Aegeus his son's fate, and those who are informed about the connection between smoking and lung cancer are under an obligation to disseminate their intelligence among those who are not, in order to enable them to act autonomously.

This notion of obligation needs expanding. Thus far we have assumed that, in a society made up of more than a Robinson Crusoe, individual autonomy cannot properly be exercised without a recognition of the role of others. You enable me to exercise my autonomy, where the circumstances require it, by providing me with necessary and appropriate information. Clearly, if I am concerned about my own autonomy, and if the exercise of my autonomy requires action on your part, then I have some interest in you. But if my interest in you were restricted to your value to me – if, in other words, I treated you purely as a means towards the satisfaction of my ends – then your interest in me would be likely to evaporate. And if I myself am to be autonomous, I must treat you as an autonomous being and provide you with whatever you require in order to exercise your autonomy. Such a pattern of mutal respect presupposes a society of reciprocally autonomous beings, each of whom has an obligation to provide the necessary wherewithal for the exercise of that of others. In fulfilling this obligation, they thereby ensure their own autonomy.

But is this not liable to lead to conflict? How can I be sure that my exercise of autonomy will not result in the curtailing of yours? We can respond to this objection by pointing out that autonomy and emotions such as care and concern are integrally related. Not only must I myself attempt to act autonomously; I must treat others as autonomous too. I must care not only about the conditions that enable them to realize their autonomy, but about their autonomy. I must treat them as though they were autonomous – a process in which care and concern for others are inevitably brought to bear in the relationship.

Why Autonomy?

This defence of autonomy against feminist criticism of its supposed individualism presupposes that autonomy is an important value. But why should one be autonomous? Is it possible to defend autonomy absolutely? Kant argues that autonomy is intimately related to personhood. It is logically impossible, he says, for an individual to contract to give up his or her rights since such a contract would deprive that person of the ability to make any contracts at all. A. Kulfik questions Kant's assertion:

> the argument falters on a temporal equivocation. Up to the moment that the contract is made, or more accurately is to take effect, the agent retains both his status as a person and whatever rights this entails, including the right to make a contract. Only after the contract takes effect does the agent (putatively) 'cease to be a person'.[5]

I agree with Kulfik that it is not actually impossible to contract to give up one's autonomy, but I do not think that Kant's argument can be so easily disposed of. Who, in their right mind, would voluntarily relinquish something if it would result in the loss of their personhood? Who, if they recognized and understood the consequences of their actions, would choose such a course? Perhaps only those for whom life itself had ceased to be worth living. Of course, if such people did not recognize the consequences of their actions, they might choose to do it, but this illustrates Kant's point. If a person did not know the consequences of giving up their autonomy, it is still the consequence – the loss of personhood – which makes the relinquishing of autonomy wrong.

It has been argued recently, however, that it must be rational for a person to give up their autonomy under certain circumstances.[6] It is reasonable, for instance, to take orders from a competent doctor in a course of treatment. In another example, two people may have conflicting beliefs about which course of action to take. Since it may not be possible for both sets of belief to be realized, it may be rational for one person to give up his or her autonomy.

As far as the first case is concerned, part of the process of rational reflection on a set of moral principles and courses of action for myself will involve consulting others (the experts, if you like). Deferring to a doctor is not in itself tantamount to accepting a view against my will, and therefore need not involve the loss of autonomy. The same point applies to the second case. We argued that I must treat other people's wants and needs as constraints on the satisfaction of my own. In other words, the rational being who is autonomously evaluating the most appropriate courses of action for herself must consider the wants, needs and interests of others. The non-satisfaction of my wants, needs, etc., is not always a violation of my autonomy. Autonomy involves the right and the capacity to exercise choice and to make reasoned judgements, and not the capacity to have those judgements invariably realized in action. The dictator (to borrow one of Keith Graham's examples) who allowed everyone to decide for themselves what they wanted, and then told them what they must do, is violating their autonomy not because their wants and needs are not realized, but because they have been coerced into doing something they do not want. In yet another sense, then, care and concern for others enters into autonomy.

Conceivably, there may be cases in which it is acceptable for someone willingly to allow themselves to be treated as a means. If, for instance, I volunteered to give up some of my bone marrow to save a person suffering from leukemia, so long as my own health was not in danger there would seem to be nothing wrong with momentarily relinquishing my autonomy. Perhaps we should draw a distinction between voluntary acts of becoming a means to the satisfaction of someone else's needs, and the involuntary treatment of an individual as a means to the satisfaction of someone else's desires. Could we then argue that only in the former case could a violation of autonomy be justified? Or is there nothing wrong in a person voluntarily allowing themselves to be treated as a means to the satisfaction of someone else's desires? If de Sade's innocent heroine Justine willingly submitted, what is wrong with her allowing herself to be treated in whatever fashion her persecutors wanted? I shall argue later that such treatment is not wrong *per se* but it is none the less wrong. In the meantime, however, we ought to examine the circumstances in which autonomy could reasonably be overruled. Richard Lindley offers a hypothetical case worthy of our careful consideration.[7]

Suppose you live in a country with a very authoritarian government and a biased press, television and radio. Elections, however, are still held, and you believe that it would be much better for the electorate if your party were in power. In order to convince the electorate of this, you would have to lie somewhat about the conditions that would follow the election of your party. You believe that your party would better promote autonomy in the long term, but you might have to violate some people's autonomy in the short term in order to further that aim. Could one, Lindley asks, justify killing soldiers who support the tyrant in order to further the long-term aim of pursuing autonomy? He suggests that 'a strict Kantian' might justify their deaths: one might say that the soldiers loyal to the tyrant were not acting autonomously in defending their tyrant, so 'thwarting their will would not be a violation of their autonomy.'[8] This would be 'consistent with the plausible view that it is not wrong to prevent someone from acting wrongly.' But, Lindley says, the 'Kantian equation of autonomy with pure rationality is questionable.' And very few people do act from pure Kantian motives, 'so interpreting the Kantian principle in this way would sanction such a widespread disregard of people's projects, as to make the principle almost vacuous in practice.' In other words, as we saw in the discussion of freedom of speech and its attempted denial to fascists, two wrongs do not make a right. Killing the soldiers is violating their autonomy.

Another Kantian strategy, Lindley suggests, 'might be to argue that the principle [of autonomy] really applies only to those who accept it, as part of a mutually binding contract.' The tyrants forfeit their right to autonomy because they fail to recognize the autonomy of others. Lindley objects to this formulation because it would wrongfully exclude young children from treatment as autonomous beings. There are further difficulties. What if, he suggests, the establishment of a new government intent on increasing autonomy led to armed conflict and the deaths of innocent people? Lindley says that this is wrong only if absolute pacifism is wrong. On the other hand, Lindley argues, there are cases – for instance where the only way to prevent a psychopathic killer from committing further murders is to kill him – in which absolute pacifism does not appear to be a justifiable moral position. He concludes, and I concur with his conclusion, that it is impossible to defend autonomy absolutely.[9]

The position I would like to defend is this: there are three and only three circumstances in which one is justified in removing a person's autonomy absolutely (by absolutely I mean by killing them, allowing them to die when their death would have been preventable, or rendering them incapable of exercising their autonomy in the future by, for instance, making them a slave). One can remove autonomy in order to promote it in the long term (as in the Lindley case described above), in order to save other lives, or because the person concerned has expressly wished that one should, because after rational deliberation, and, in the absence of constraints, they had decided that their life had ceased to be worth living. Otherwise, I would argue, there is a premium on maximizing autonomy in any one individual, and on spreading autonomy as widely as possible in the wider community.

The view I have been defending here is a form of moral neutralism. In the previous chapter, I put forward the view that moral neutralism sometimes appears to be indefensible. Individuating facts about people such as their colour or sex may be morally relevant. None the less, we can see that one form of moral neutralism is correct.

Bernard Williams argues that moral neutralism is a goal that makes no sense: agent-relative concerns are, in the end, what gives life its meaning.[10] For example, he says, it is absurd to do what neutralist morality requires, and save two strangers from drowning in preference to one's spouse. Commitments to friends, family, etc., are, he argues, what give life its meaning. One cannot be as deeply committed to the neutralist goals of promoting autonomy, freedom, etc.

I would argue that it is not morally wrong to save one's spouse at the expense of the two strangers. Similarly, it would not be wrong, if one were black and identified with black people, to save a black person at the expense of two whites. In these cases, the dividing line between the requirements of a neutralist morality and those of the agent-relative one are fine: one has a choice between saving two strangers or one's spouse. But suppose that the choice was between saving ten strangers or one's spouse. In this case, I think, one's feelings – the area of life, which, according to Williams, gives it 'substance' – would be affected. Whereas one could (perhaps) go through life having failed to save two strangers, it would be harder to do so if one had failed to save ten people. Compare this with, for instance, a choice between saving one's own life on a sinking ship and making a bridge from the ship onto a life boat oneself (at considerable risk to one's own life) in order to save other lives. Our 'feelings' would go out to the one who risked her own life. We can allow 'agent-relative' concerns to intervene in considering the morally correct thing to do, but the overriding principle is the moral-neutralist commitment to goals independently of the person to whom they apply.

Williams argues that we cannot have the same commitment to morally neutral goals such as the pursuit of autonomy as we do to personal goals. I would question this assertion. One can, after all, develop commitments to all sorts of things in addition to, or instead of, one's family and friends. People get committed to computing or chess, pursuing political ends or just to arguing. Those who pursue these ends at the expense of goals like family and friends might be labelled 'eccentric', but the labelling does not show their actions to be morally wrong. Why should we not develop commitments as strong as those towards our friends to the morally neutral goals of pursuing autonomy?

Up to a point, then, moral neutralism is correct. As we have seen, however, our moral ontology is not just made up of individuals. There are also collectives, and this affects our view of moral neutralism. Where it is a question of absolute removal of autonomy (by death or slavery) one cannot promote the interests of collectives over and above the autonomy of individuals. It is not justifiable, for instance, to promote the interests of black people (even though black people have been discriminated against in the past) by eliminating the autonomy of whites; removing autonomy altogether is justified only in the very special circumstances to which we have already alluded. But the removal of white autonomy would not, in the end, promote the interests of blacks. Suppose, for instance, a black liberation group was urging that the best means of promoting its interests was the elimination of white people. (This same view, albeit of men, is advocated by the extreme 'feminist' group SCUM.) This action would not be in the interests of black people, because it is unlikely that it could be carried out without generating the belief among black people that it is acceptable to eliminate one group in the interests of another.

It would, however, be consistent with the position advocated in the last chapter to argue that it is alright to curtail the autonomy of one black or indeed one white person in order to propagate the interests of black people as a whole. If that one person was promoting views which ran contrary to the interests of the group, that person could be censored. Thus there are circumstances in which moral neutralism with regard to individuals might be overridden; 'agent-specific' concerns might assume greater importance than morally neutral goals where the 'agent' is not an individual but a group. In such circumstances, I would argue, it might be right to override moral neutralism with regard to individuals. Thus, where the interests of collectives are concerned, the presumption in favour of maximizing autonomy in individuals, and spreading it as evenly as possible, may be overridden.

Conclusion

Far from being 'individualist', autonomy requires a commitment to one form of non-individualism – the values of care and concern for others. Consistently with the argument of the last chapter we can therefore defend the morally neutral goal of promoting autonomy. But, as I have argued, we cannot be committed to autonomy absolutely: rather, one ought to maximize it in individuals and the community. This position, however, is open to qualification when one considers the viewpoint of collectives. Sometimes, I have suggested, the interests of the collective may override the autonomy of the individual (although, I suggested, one is not justified, save in very special circumstances, in removing the autonomy of an individual absolutely).

This chapter concludes my critique of the liberal/individualist perspective. In these first four chapters, while I have criticized one aspect in particular of the liberal tradition – its individualism – I have defended some of its values – notably autonomy and liberty – and argued that the full realization of these values demands a non-individualistic perspective.

I have argued that the liberal individualist commitment to the freedom of the individual obscures the power relations in the production and consumption of porn. I have not mentioned the subject of pornography in this chapter. We will see, however, that this chapter has provided an important contribution to our understanding of what is wrong with pornography.

5
Dworkin:
Male Power and Violence

Most of the discussion so far has been centred on the liberal position on pornography as enunciated by the Williams Report. I have argued that though certain of its values are important, its individualistic premises are wrong and misleading and that its underlying focus on people as equal, rational beings fails to give proper credence to the fact that it is mainly women who are depicted in many pornographic magazines, and mainly men who produce and consume them. These facts come very much to the fore in radical feminist readings of pornography.

My discussion of radical feminist treatments of pornography focuses almost entirely on published work, and on a restricted sample of radical feminist writing at that. It must be acknowledged that this runs the risk of failing to do justice to the activist side of radical feminism. Furthermore, the selection of writers is largely a personal choice, although I have tried to pick out those radical feminist writers whose work is most influential, in the UK and the USA.

A number of radical feminists believe that pornography lies at the heart of women's oppression. Pornographic depictions of women, they say, serve to create and sustain patriarchal social relations, relations in which men dominate women. Their strong views on pornography are fuelled by their perception that women in porn are mutilated and subjected to violence in particularly horrific ways. In the end, they would argue, it is heterosexual sexual relations themselves which lie at the root of women's subordination; pornography is merely the starkest illustration of how heterosexual sex reinforces men's violent behaviour.

The United States Supreme Court recently ruled unconstitutional a state ordinance in Indianapolis which claimed that pornography violates women's civil rights. The ruling and the ordinance, based on a model drafted by Catherine MacKinnon and Andrea Dworkin for Minneapolis,[1] has generated controversy among American feminists. Adrienne Rich, for instance, has signed a brief arguing against the Indianapolis ordinance.

The background to the controversy is Andrea Dworkin's book *Pornography: Men Possessing Women*, in which she presents a powerful and vividly illustrated case to the effect that porn is at the centre of male supremacy. For Dworkin, the subordination of women means male power. This 'power of men', she believes, is manifested in various ways. First, 'the power of men is ... a metaphysical assertion of self ... It expresses intrinsic authority ...'[2] 'Men,' she says, 'have this self and ... women must by definition lack it.'[3] Secondly, 'power is physical strength used over and against others less strong or without the sanction to use strength as power.'[4] Dworkin refers to women's weakness both in the physical sense and in terms of their role in 'the male system'. 'Even women who are physically strong', she submits, 'must pretend to be weak to underline ... their femininity ... Physical incapacity is a form of feminine beauty ...'[5] The reality or myth of male physical strength, she believes, is and must be sanctioned by law and by culture: 'Laws and customs protect it; art and literature adore it; history depends on it; ... it is not a subjective phenomenon; its significance is not whimsical.' For Dworkin, this second tenet of male supremacy combines with the first, so that the man 'not only is, he is stronger, he not only takes, he takes by force.'[6] The third aspect of male power is men's

> capacity to terrorize, to use self and strength to inculcate fear, fear *in* a whole class of persons *of* a whole class of persons. The acts of terror run the gamut from rape to battery to sexual abuse of children to war to murder to maiming to torture to enslaving to kidnapping to verbal assault to cultural assault to threats of death to threats of harm backed up by the ability and sanction to deliver.

Terror, she thinks, 'issues forth from the male, illuminates his essential nature and his basic purpose.'[7]

At times Dworkin appears to believe that the male is a terrorizer 'by nature': 'men are biologically aggressive ...' Elsewhere, however, she advances the view that biological theory is itself part of the 'male supremacist legend'. Thus, according to this position, the science of biology, presumably along with the other sciences, is geared towards shoring up the male system. Moreover, for Dworkin, 'men have the power of naming.' This power enables them 'to define experience, to articulate boundaries and values, to designate to each thing its realm and qualities, to determine what can and cannot be expressed, to control perception itself'. 'Male supremacy',

Dworkin says, 'is fused into the language so that every sentence both heralds and affirms it.'[8] Men both maintain their power of naming through force and 'justify force through the power of naming'. For instance, 'the male does not merely name women evil; he exterminates nine million women as witches because he has named women evil.'[9]

Another male power is 'the power of owning'. Men own women and children. This practice, according to her, persists even today; in the US, though the letter of the law denies men this ownership, its spirit does not. 'Wife beating and marital rape, pervasive here as elsewhere, are predicated on the conviction that a man's ownership of his wife licenses whatever he wished to do to her ...'[10] This right of the male to own the woman 'is presumed natural'; it is derived from the first tenet of male supremacy. Finally, 'men have the power of sex.' Sex becomes defined by the male as sexual colonization. The real meaning of 'male supremacy' is taking and possessing women.

Sexuality is implied in some of her other definitions of male power. For instance, in discussing the capacity to terrorize, Dworkin says that the penis is a symbol of terror 'even more significant ... the gun, the knife, the bomb, the fist, and so on.'[11] The core of the male power of naming, for her, is the male naming the woman as sex object and raping her. 'Owning' has sexual connotations; the man owns the woman so that he can use her sexually. Even money is sexual: 'the power of money is used by men to buy women and sex.' 'Money is primary in the acquisition of sex and sex is primary in the making of money ...'[12] Even where sex is not explicitly mentioned, it is implicit in Dworkin's description of the nature of male power. It is in the very air we breathe: 'male sexual power', she says, 'is the substance of culture.'[13]

According to Dworkin, sexuality is at the root of male supremacy, of male power. Additionally, male supremacy, or women's subordination has to do with violence against women. A central part of women's subordination is their role as the objects of male violence. Thus both sexuality and violence are at the core of male power. Male sexuality is violent sexuality; heterosexual sex is tantamount to violence perpetrated against women:

> saber penetrating a vagina is a weapon; so is the camera or the pen that renders it; so is the penis for which it substitutes (vagina literally means 'sheath'). The persons who produce the image are also weapons as men deployed in war become in their persons

weapons. Those who defend or protect the image are, in this same sense, weapons.[14]

The little boy, according to Dworkin, is a parasite who drains and destroys any potential autonomy his mother might have. Men mutilate women either physically – by battering or rape – or by fashion and custom, so that physical strength becomes unnecessary. The terror that men use against women – raping and battering women, sexually abusing children – is different only in degree from the terror inflicted by maiming and torturing in warfare.

So far we can see two fundamental aspects of male power over women. Women are the objects of male violence and this violence is mainly expressed sexually. But the vehicle used by the male colonizers to exercise their domination over their female territories is pornography. 'These strains of male power are intrinsic to both the substance and production of pornography, and the ways and means of pornography are the ways and means of male power.'[15] All the forms of male power are discernible in porn. Male power is manifested not just in the form and content of porn, but also in the 'economic control and distribution of wealth within the industry'. The women represented in pornographic pictures are 'objects', the photographer or writer is an 'aggressor', and 'the critic or intellectual who through naming assigns value in the application of material in what is called real life',[16] embodies male power.

Porn, then, becomes the major agent reproducing male power and women's subordination. Dworkin vividly describes a number of pornographic pictures that exemplify male power. In one photo, called 'Beaver Hunters', two white men dressed as hunters sit in a black jeep.

> The Jeep occupies almost the whole frame of the picture. The two men carry rifles. The rifles extend above the frame of the photograph into the white space surrounding it. The men and the Jeep face into the camera. Tied onto the hood of the black Jeep is a white woman. She is tied with thick rope. She is spread-eagle. Her pubic hair and crotch are the dead center of the car hood and the photograph ... The men in the photo are self-possessed; that is, they possess the power of self ... They are armed: first in the sense that they are fully clothed; second, because they carry rifles, which are made more prominent, suggesting erection ... The woman is possessed; that is, she has no self ...[17]

The photo celebrates the physical power of man over woman ...[18]

Dworkin believes that the subordination of women means male power, primarily male sexual power over women, and that this power is expressed violently. An additional part of her thesis is that the major agent reproducing this power is pornography. Porn does this because it is the paradigm case of the exercise of violent sexual power over women; it is 'the graphic depiction of women as vile whores.'

Dworkin is not alone in this view. For instance in a paper written for the London Regional Revolutionary Feminist Conference, a feminist asks, 'How is it possible to study the effects of total immersion from birth in a pornographic society?'[19] In *Take Back the Night: Women on Pornography,* Irene Diamond writes: 'the "what" of porn is power and violence and the "who" of concern is women.'[20] Sheila Jeffreys gives a suggestion for action:

> If all women decided that porn should not exist and smashed and destroyed it on news stands, bill boards, in the windows of sex shops, on the streets of Soho, and demanded their right never to be insulted in public again, then at least it would be a beginning since the end of the struggle could only be the destruction of male supremacy itself.[21]

But where Dworkin believes that porn *is* violence against women. others contend that it *causes* violence. The American radical feminist Robin Morgan, for example, adopted a slogan since taken up by British women's groups: 'Porn is the theory; rape is the practice.' Once more pornography emerges as a major agent of the reproduction of women's subordination.

I disagree with these feminists. I believe that Dworkin is wrong about male power, and that porn does not play the role she believes it does in reproducing women's subordination. Let me begin by discussing her view of the nature of male power.

Male Power and Violence

Male power, for Dworkin, is expressed violently. Certainly, the violence committed by men against women must not be underestimated.

At the end of 1980, two women in Leeds were sentenced to three years' imprisonment for killing their father in self-defence. He was, it appeared, so violent that the police had been called to their home many times, and he had been barred from pubs for two miles around.[22] Peter Sutcliffe, the Yorkshire ripper, killed thirteen

young women. If we are to believe the recent Cleveland statistics
in the UK, and other evidence, incest – usually by fathers, uncles,
friends, grandfathers – against young girls, is legion.

Dworkin argues that such incidents are part of a pattern, making
violence against women the core of male power. For her, male
violence is not restricted to physical activities like rape, warfare
and wife-beating. The force of subjection is also psychic and social.
The 'power' of naming is one that is imposed on women, by men,
invading their souls. In common with other feminists of the 1980s
(Daly and Brownmiller, to mention but two), Dworkin sees male
power as unitary. In the 1970s and earlier, feminists tended to view
women's oppression as a diverse phenomenon, manifested in
different ways in the workplace, in the streets and in the home.
The sources of male power lay, according to many feminist writers
of the period, in the major institutions of contemporary capitalism,
in 'the military, industry, technology, universities, science, political
office and finance.'[23] Force was not the crucial manifestation of
male power. Later in the 1970s, however, particularly in the USA,
rape began to be seen as the issue uniting all feminists: it was seen
to symbolize women's vulnerability to men. A woman could be
raped at any time, therefore all women's lives were seen to be
controlled by this threat. As one pair of writers put it:

> It is not rape itself which constitutes a form of social control, but
> the internalisation by women ... of the possibility of rape. This
> implicit threat of rape is conveyed in terms of certain
> prescriptions which are placed upon the behaviour of girls and
> women, and through the commonsense understandings which
> 'naturalise' gender appropriate forms of behaviour.[24]

In the 1980s feminists like Mary Daly and Andrea Dworkin came to
see male violence as lying at the core of women's subordination, as
the unifying factor in such apparently disparate phenomena as
employers' exploitation of women workers and the harassment of
wives by husbands. But what exactly does Dworkin understand by
'violence'? What is the connection between sex and violence?

One claim is that 'the penis' is a symbol of terror. Although I
agree that there is such a thing as symbolic violence, the
appropriateness of Dworkin's symbols is questionable. We can
accept, for instance, that the Nazi salute is a symbol of violence,
because its cultural meaning is inextricably associated with Nazi
behaviour towards Jews, gays, etc. But why should the penis play a
corresponding role? Because of its shape? Because it penetrates a

woman? Perhaps, more plausibly, because it is the tool used in the act of rape? But aren't we now talking about a symbolic penis? Aren't we referring, not to the floppy appendage, but to the phallus – the physical organ represented as continuously erect? Aren't we referring to the penis as represented in hard-porn magazines? Real penises, most of the time, are rather soft, tender and squashy. Why should these appendages attached to real men who can often be loving, caring and tender, symbolize violence? Certainly it is true in our patriarchal culture that little boys tend to learn violent behaviour; that men often behave violently towards women, and that masculinity is symbolically associated with myths of aggression. Buy why has the penis been chosen to symbolize these cultural facts? Why not instead a hairy, muscular body, arm outstretched and fingers clenched? Why not a hairy leg kicking? Why choose the penis, and then suggest that the capacity to penetrate the woman turns the penis into a weapon? 'A saber penetrating a vagina is a *weapon* ... but so is the penis for which it substitutes.'[25]

Heterosexual sex can be loving, caring and warm. A saber penetrating a vagina could never be any of these things. Penises are not sabers. Nazi salutes symbolize complicity with those who are prepared to kill Jewish people: the salute has no meaning or function independently of its symbolic role. Penises are different: of themselves they do not symbolize anything. Only as 'the phallus', erect and hard, can the penis symbolize the violent aspects of partriachy. But even representing the abundance and inexhaustable quality of male desire, its link with violence is tenuous. For many women, an erect penis has no connection with violence: 'The one time I did fuck with Charles, it felt really *good*, like there was an awful lot that was important going on.'[26] 'I feel a riot of conflicting emotions. One quite simple one is that I want him – I just want him. I want to be with him and sleep with him.'[27]

Women's fear and men's aggression then, are not reasons to label the penis a symbol of violence. Moreover, as Ellen Willis has pointed out, there is a problem with Dworkin's connection between sex and violence. 'If', she says, 'all manifestations of sexuality are violent, then opposition to violence cannot explain why pornography ... should be singled out as a target.'[28] Suppose instead that we interpret Dworkin along the lines of a suggestion from Smart and Smart – that women's behaviour in general is partly conditioned by the threat of rape, thus the possibility of violence constitutes, for all women, a form of social control. But is women's behaviour in general conditioned by the threat of rape? It seems highly unlikely. Even if it were, it would be far-fetched to explain other aspects of women's oppression (their average low wages relative to men's, for instance) as an effect of the power of men as potential rapists. Women's average wages are lower than men's because men tend to occupy the more powerful and the higher status positions in the workplace. This in turn is partly a consequence of gender stereotyping elsewhere. And this gender stereotyping comes about, surely, in a variety of ways, as I and others have argued elsewhere, not the least of them being the Freudian Oedipus complex, the way little boys and little girls are treated in their early years.[29] To ascribe the responsibility for low wages to men's capacity to rape women just does not ring true.

Dworkin herself clearly believes that male violence against women is primarily sexual. But implicit in her words, and much more explicit in the work of other radical feminists of the 1980s, is the idea that a very large part of the behaviour of men towards women can be described as violent. Thus, for instance, some British revolutionary feminists, writing in the collection *Women Against Violence Against Women*,[29] suggest that some words used by men may suggest or symbolize violence. Words like rape, murder, etc., carry violence on their sleeves, as it were. Caroline Ramazanoglu makes a similar point in her article 'Sex and Violence in Academic Life'.[30] Ramazanoglu suggests that verbal techniques such as the powerful use of the voice 'to convey sarcasm, to interrupt, to prevent interruption and to override counter-arguments'[31] constitute verbal forms of intimidation that can be described as violent. She is concerned particularly with their use by academics (usually male) in positions of power over students. But her point could be generalized to apply to language use more generally.

The difficulty with describing these verbal techniques as constituting evidence of male violence against women is that they may be, and often are, used by women against men. Although in *Man Made Language* Dale Spender offers evidence which suggests that they are used more by men than by women, the evidence is not sufficient to justify the claim that the phenomenon is specifically a male one.[32]

Furthermore, describing this form of verbal behaviour as violent may defuse one's very proper negative reaction to violent acts like rape and murder. The legal systems of the USA and UK were just beginning, in the mid-1980s, to recognize and express horror at the violent crime of rape. If judges are also expected by the very feminists who are beginning to persuade them of the horrors of rape, to show horror and deal appropriately with cases of verbal abuse, their reaction to rape may be weakened.

Many feminists would, no doubt, argue that those judges are wrong, and must be so persuaded. Examining cases of verbal violence in the courts might lead them to think more deeply about physical violence, rather than anaesthetizing them to it. Feminists, after all, are waging a multifaceted campaign. But let us recall the literal meaning of the word 'violent': 'the exercise of physical force so as to inflict injury or damage on a person or property' (OED). Rape is violent according to this definition, yet it is itself only at a rudimentary stage in being treated as such in most courts. Would it not be premature and misguided to ask the very same judges to consider simultaneously cases which are not clearly characterizable as 'violent'? To demand both that rape be recognized as the violent crime that it is and that verbal techniques also be seen to be violent is to ask to have one's cake and eat it too.

Of course there are metaphorical uses of the word 'violent', as in a violent noise or a violent colour, but feminists like Ramazanoglu surely intend to imply a stronger-than-metaphorical sense for the term. She would like techniques such as academics' use of the voice to convey sarcasm to be seen as violent in some similar sense to acts like rape. But what is this sense? The crucial element of physical force is lacking in the former. We might plausibly refer to psychological intimidation, but why should we stop there? Why not call emotional intimidation – such as that exercised by a small boy over his mother – violent? But then it is once more difficult to describe violence as a male phenomenon, since many acts of emotional intimidation are carried out by girls against fathers.

Another WAVAW feminist, writing in the collection: *Women Against Violence Against Women*, argues that 'fashion' can constitute 'violence against women'.[33] 'Everyday women suffer an immense amount of pain through diets (anorexia and compulsive eating), plastic surgery, hair removal (electrolysis, depilatories, waxing), the list is endless. Women are being taught to be alienated from their bodies and other women's bodies.'[34] As it stands, this does not prove any link between fashion and violence: a woman can suffer pain – from her periods, as a result of falling over in the street, etc. – when the cause has nothing to do with her being the object of violence at all, let alone male violence. Expanding on the idea, however, one might argue that violence is done to the female body by restricting it and shaping it in accordance with the dictates (a term with possibly violent connotations) of fashion. These dictates have their origin in an image over which women have no control. One might say that men, as a group, are responsible for this state of affairs. But the arguments I put against language being described as violent apply here too. If fashion is violent, then one is left at a loss to explain why it is that a man raping a woman is worse than a woman's wearing the latest fashions. It is, surely, worse precisely because the former involves violence. The generalizing of the term numbs one's feelings against rape/wife beating, etc. In another context, the feminist biologist Ruth Bleier[35] argues that it is misleading to label the fertilization by a male plant of a female one as rape (as some feminists have done) because the act has a quite different point and purpose. I suggest that it is misleading, too, to label all actions for which men could be said to be responsible, and in which women are the targets, as violent.

Historically, male power has appeared in ways that have nothing whatsoever to do with treating women violently. Here, power means men's ability – whether exercised consciously or not – to control women. Male power appears, for instance, in the representation of women as good, innocent, pretty, virginal and blonde: the Marquis de Sade's Justine; the Marilyn Monroe of *Gentlemen Prefer Blondes*. The power of men is evident in Jane Austen's *Sensibility*, and in the heroines of many an historical romance. The Virgin Mary (who combines the ability to give birth and to mother with the innocence of the virgin), the Greek goddess Artemis, and her Roman counterpart Diana (the goddess of the morning, forests, animals and women in childbirth) provide some of the strongest evidence of male power. Male power also appears in the representation of women at the opposite extreme, as the whore: de Sade's Juliette, and the 'bad black woman'.[36]

What do I mean by saying that these various representations of women all provide evidence of male power? How can the depiction of a woman by a woman count as yet more evidence of the phenomenon? The answer is that men, on the whole, have been responsible for creating these images, and they have done so in order to maintain their superiority over women. I do not mean that each individual man has thought up the idea, and has intentionally set out to do women down. Rather, men as a group are responsible, in the way that the jury in Chapter 3 was responsible, for creating and sustaining these conceptions.

Women writers internalize male values about women, and present them as though they were their own. Jane Austen, George Eliot and Charlotte Lamb (a Mills and Boon author) all do this to varying degrees. (Which is not to say that their books do not contain, at the same time, material that contributes to cracking the cement in the edifice of male power.)

Dworkin's exclusive focus on violence as the root of women's subordination, and her (in my view) illegitimate extension of the meaning of the word 'violent', may ironically be downplaying other aspects of male power. A critic can easily say: *those* acts are not violent, therefore there is nothing wrong with them. Additionally, Dworkin's tendency to blame individual men for the power of men as a group – 'he's a man, he's got to be violent' (compare: 'she's white, therefore she's racist') – underemphasizes the extent to which it is difficult, if not impossible, for individual men to fit the image of the powerful, macho, masculine male. How many men can possibly live up to the James Bond image, with four near escapes from death before breakfast, and a beautiful blonde, dumb woman in tow? How many men would enjoy being heroes of the Falklands or of the American contras in Nicaragua? Few men are masters and heroes like the warriors of the ancient Greek city states. Few fit the description of 'stud', 'stallion', 'beef' or 'cock'. Few live up to the image of the man as logical, rational, non-emotional and hard.

Dworkin's picture also obscures the fact that there has been racism towards other men in some of the images of masculinity – of the powerful male. Man as 'reasonable, logical and thoughtful', as Paul Hoch points out, is the white hero; man as 'virile and aggressive' is the 'black beast'. St George, the white hero, triumphs over the dragon (the black beast); Othello, a black man, is 'a barbarian'; and nineteenth-century white Europe subdues Africa. The epithet 'an old black ram' is not adequately spelt out as 'a violent and powerful man'.

Dworkin's view further tends to downplay class differences between men. Any unitary analysis of 'male power' obliterates the fact that some men have power over others: Rupert Murdoch over most journalists; the factory managers over their workforce. Any power that a poor working-class man has over Princess Diana must be of a different order from that exerted by the factory manager over his wife.

Some have argued that the consumption of pornography among working-class men can be explained as the result of their powerlessness. Lawrence Rosenfield[37] and David Chute argue that the use of pornography is a symptom of men's powerlessness.[38] The traditional image of the user of pornography – the middle-aged man in the trench coat masturbating into his hat – is the powerful man at his nadir.[39] Alan Soble[40] expands on Rosenfield and Chute's analysis: in capitalist societies, he says, 'commodification' is the universal structuring principle. The fetishization of commodities has repercussions in the spheres both of production and of reproduction.

Capitalist production is predominantly production for exchange value. In capitalist modes of production, labour power becomes a commodity. Men, Soble argues, tend to be associated more than women with the sphere of production. There is a corresponding disposition for women to be confined to the reproductive sphere. The role of the productive labourer, Soble argues, desensitizes the male body. Capitalism further encourages the 'commodification' of sexuality. Women, through working more in the sphere of reproduction, or at least in 'nurturing' and service industries, are less infected and influenced by the commodity form. Capitalism also encourages the commodification of women's bodies, and pornography is used by men to satisfy their alienated sexuality, in the capitalist mode of production. In making sexual arousal a commodity, pornography replicates the commodification of women's bodies. Soble concludes that in capitalist societies, the consumption of porn, far from being a symptom of male power, is precisely an effect of working-class men's powerlessness. In his article 'Pornography', Andy Moye[41] makes a similar point. He describes the 'phallic desire' implicit in much porn as 'alienated work'. In using porn, men are alienated from pleasure.

Soble, however, has not sufficiently extricated himself from the generalizing models of Dworkin et al. It is difficult to believe that capitalism affects all men in the same sort of way, from labourers on the factory floor to office workers to MPs. Most women, in any event, are not confined to the sphere of reproduction. Working in the service industries does not exempt one from the objectifying, alienating side of the capitalist mode of production. Moreover, one could argue that the concentration of female workers in less skilled, lower paid occupations[42] would lead to some women's sexuality being more alienated than men's. One final point: Geoffrey Gorer[43] argues that many wealthy Victorians consumed porn. Surely, on Soble's argument, one would expect precisely the opposite to be true.

In fact, most of Soble's arguments suffer from a similar weakness to those of Dworkin. They assume the 'male' role, on the one hand, and the female one, on the other, to be unitary. To say that the consumption of pornography results from 'men's powerlessness' suffers from the same kind of over-generalization as Dworkin's thesis. Indeed, Dworkin's generalizing perspective has more legitimacy than Soble's, since she is looking for a unitary feature to explain a general phenomenon, women's oppression by men. But Soble is setting out to explain a phenomenon that is far less widespread – the consumption of porn by men in capitalism – by reference to a generalization about men in capitalism. A large number of men in capitalism do not consume porn.

Despite my reservations about these arguments, however, my objections to Dworkin remain. The feminists of the 1970s were, I believe, correct to argue that male power is a diffuse phenomenon, although it could no doubt be given a unitary analysis. But I also disagree with Dworkin about the role played by porn in reproducing women's subordination. In order to clarify the nature of my disagreement, I'll look at two further aspects of the views of Dworkin and others: first, the assertion that porn is violence against women and second, the claim that porn causes violence against women.

Porn is Violence Against Women

Can pornography be described as violent? Almost all pornographic material is representational. If it is violent, it represents or depicts violence. It might, like Plato's poets, depict violence at several removes: it portrays representation of violence. Plenty of porn portrays real, and not merely symbolic, violence. 'Snuff' movies end in the horrific mutilation and murder of the 'heroine'. A recent hard-core video from Denmark, *The Story of Joanna*, shows a macho, dominant male who gets the woman to act out his wishes and fantasies. He fucks her so that the act is painful to her, beats her and ties her up. The film ends with the woman murdering the man, but this seems metaphorical only: the actual violence throughout is perpetrated by the man against the woman. Susan Griffin cites the film *Peeping Tom*, whose hero is a pornographic photographer.[44] As he photographs a woman, his camera releases a spear which 'simultaneously murders her'. Thus he murders her as he makes her into an image 'and replaces her body with a record of her death agony'. The film *Dressed to Kill* showed women being assaulted, raped and murdered. Andrea Dworkin's book itself is packed with vivid descriptions of particularly nasty pieces of porn. Many hard-core porn magazines contain pictures of women chained and tied, ready for the male to perform his will upon them.

Outside the realm of the magazine and the video we see similar themes. In Norman Mailer's *The American Dream*, the hero kills his wife and cries out 'release'. The inspiration for these horrors is, of course, the Marquis de Sade's *Justine*, the story of the innocent virgin who is subjected to an horrific array of tortures and rapes, who is convicted and sentenced for crimes not only that she did not commit, but which, indeed, were perpetrated against her.

Many recent feminist writers see violent porn as typical. Thus Polly Toynbee in her *Guardian* column in 1981 made this observation: 'Scenes of torture, castration, flogging, cannibalism, the crushing of breasts in vices, exploding vaginas packed with hand grenades, eyes gouged out, beatings, dismemberings, burnings, multiple rape ...'[45] Sally Wagner too sees male violence as an 'ever-present potential in porn, waiting to make its appearance.'[46] Kathleen Barry describes pornography as 'female sexual slavery and cultural sadism'. 'SM', she says, 'is not just a weird, fringe sex cult. It is in. It is romance.'[47] The pornography of cultural sadism, she suggests, has permeated the whole of society.

However, while hard-core porn is more readily available in the US and the rest of Europe than in Britain, in both the US and Britain, according to national readership surveys, the most widely read male porn magazines are *Mayfair*, *Penthouse*, *Playboy* and *Men Only*. (These, incidentally, have a smaller readership among the male populace than thrillers.) These four magazines have a combined 1.6 to 2 million (mainly male) readers per average issue. *Penthouse* has the largest circulation of all, with peak sales in 1976. These magazines supply a basic 'diet of titillation' to the average reader. Each magazine contains a collection of glossy photographs of one or more girls (the age of the woman photographed usually runs between 18 and 20 with a few a little older) clad either in nothing at all, or in nothing but leather boots and long gloves, or just tiny panties. Alongside these pictures is a short biography of the girl in question (so that the reader can feel he 'knows' her). For instance: 'For pet of the month Linda Keaton, beauty's not only an asset and a blessing but also her business' (*Penthouse*). Or, '"Sex is the most important thing in my life", says Sybil' (*Playboy*). 'Generally speaking, girls comes in two types and sizes. There are the tall, cool and sophisticated ones, and the small, cute and bouncy ones. If your favourite is the latter, you'll love Zoe' (*Mayfair*).

The sexism is obvious. A girl becomes like a pet cat or dog; the girls are advertised like a collection of suits or children's toys. But none of these quotes involves violence against women in any obvious sense. The women are not being physically hurt by anyone nor, indeed, are they being psychologically or emotionally intimidated. On the contrary, the women are represented as enjoying themselves, and not in a masochistic manner. This is the degradation of women, the downplaying of women's intelligence and abilities, the denial that they are real human beings, but it is not subjecting women to violence.

Moreover, these glossy photos make up only the centre pages of the magazine. There are also stories, features, problems, letters (and nowadays not all of them even involve sex). One recent *Penthouse* featured some of a cartoonist's caricatures of Thatcher, Andropov and others. Sone of the stories and cartoons even denigrate men. For instance: 'it's a beautiful honeymoon, dear, but I shall miss my vibrator' (*Playboy*). One story in a recent *Penthouse* begins in a way that would not be unacceptable in a feminist magazine. It is a story about 'Alison' who is living in a hypothetical nuclear catastrophe. Ninety-nine per cent of the males have been destroyed by radiation poisoning, and the poisoning is being repeated in male embryos. The women, however, have found a method of reproducing themselves without sperm. The precious 1 per cent of men are kept in 'male centres'. Now we come to the *Penthouse* bit: Alison is singled out for physical mating, rather than for artificial insemination. She has the honour of going to a male centre, where she is shown porn films from the world before the catastrophe. Of course she is fantastically excited by these films, and ends up 'being fucked' by two men. Clearly there is a sexism in that story. So too is there in many of the letters in the magazines (e.g. 'What's the best way to put a woman down without coming across as an insensitive snot?') However, I stress again that none of them involve violence in any of the senses I earlier described. There is no rape. There is no symbolism like the Nazi symbol. And there is no suggestion that the women are being hurt. Indeed, there are no penises or phalluses: the magazines contain, almost exclusively, pictures of women. Quite simply, the porn that is most widely disseminated, both in the US and in Britain, does not involve the representation of violence either real or symbolic, in Dworkin's sense, against women.

Even if we were to look exclusively at the hard-core porn market we would not find it dominated by images of violence. *Private*, a magazine produced by a Swede, Berthe Milton, has the highest circulation worldwide of any hard-core porn magazine. Its bi-monthly distribution is well over 100,000 copies.[48] By far the majority of the contents of this magazine (a magazine which, by repute, prides itself on its spectactular scenic settings and the quality of its photography) are scenes of heterosexual sexual intercourse. In their book *Porn Gold: Inside the Pornography Business*, Hebditch and Anning quote magazine editorials in which Milton espouses opinions that strongly oppose violence. They also cite, as an example of the vehemence of Milton's views on the subject, an issue of the magazine (*Private* No. 8, 1967) in which

Milton had published a set of four photographs:

> Three of these showed graphic acts of violence, including the
> bullet-riddled head of 1930s bank robber Clyde Barrow, the Major of
> Saigon shooting a suspected Viet Cong soldier and South Vietnamese
> special forces showing off the decapitated heads of captured
> enemy. The fourth depicts a couple engaged in sexual intercourse,
> the penetration clearly visible.[49]

The censors removed only the fourth photograph. Milton's editorial,
quoted by Hebditch and Anning, ran as follows:

> With the approval of the censoring authorities in question,
> abnormal and horrible acts of violence have been shown in the
> greater part of civilization – distributed via newspapers, magazines,
> film and television.
>   Murders and throat cuttings are obviously matters within the
> limits of decency.
>   Why is it, then, that in so many parts of the world realism in
> love-making and sexual intercourse between human beings are
> not allowed to be shown?[50]

How can the·description of *Private* as 'violent' be of any value
when its editor has proclaimed himself so strongly against the
phenomenon? Is it not possible that Dworkin has excluded the
highest circulation hard-core pornographic magazine from counting
as porn, if all porn is violent? Would not the waters be muddied,
rather than cleared, if she were to begin distinguishing senses of
the term 'violent'?

Nor could any of the porn I have described be delineated as
'cultural sadism' à la Kathleen Barry. The forms of torture fantasized
and enacted by the Marquis de Sade, and from whom we derive the
expression 'sadism' ('a form of sexual perversion marked by a love
of cruelty' – OED), are as different from the pin-ups in *Playboy* or
Penthouse as chalk from cheese. Much porn may involve treating
women as slaves (see Chapter 9), but most of it is not sadistic. Just
as it is important to reserve the word 'violent' to describe acts like
rape, torture, etc., so too ought we to classify pornography, like de
Sade's *Juliette*, which is actually sadistic, separately from porn,
which is not.

Marianne Valverde makes the point that 'to discuss porn is to
raise our consciousness about violence against women'.[51] And she
suggests that women do feel attacked and made vulnerable by

images of bound and gagged women. Both of these points are important; however, feminists may *lower* the consciousness of some people if exaggerated claims about pornography are made. The hypothetical sympathetic judge should surely not be expected to take women's outrage at the centre spread in a *Playboy* magazine as on a par with the emotions of the woman who has undergone the horrific experience of a rape. The judge's consciousness on the subject of rape might be lowered were he to be expected to do so. Violence and sadomasochism are 'crimes' of a different order from the 'objectification' of women in *Playboy*. Gayle Rubin concurs:

> Actually, if you walk into an adult bookstore, ninety per cent of the material you will see is frontal nudity, intercourse and oral sex, with no hint of violence or coercion. There are speciality porns ... and there is a genre of porn that caters to sadomasochists, which is the porn they focus on when you see a WAVPM [Women Against Violence in Pornography and the Media] or a WAP [Women Against Pornography] slide show.[52]

Dworkin's thesis is misleading, then, on several counts. First of all, the subordination of women is not equivalent to violence located in the penis and perpetrated by men. Secondly, Dworkin's symbols of violence are inappropriate. And finally, porn is not the paradigm case of the exercise of violent male sexuality because the porn that is the most heavily perused is not violent, neither actually nor symbolically in Dworkin's sense.

Porn Causes Violence Against Women

The other claim made by women who believe that porn is a major agent in the reproduction of male power is that, though porn itself may not constitute violence against women, it causes it. Sandra McNeill says: 'There is in fact evidence to suggest a strong connection between pornography and sexual violence.'[53] Porn should be condemned as a major factor in reproducing women's subordination, the argument runs, because the violence that porn brings about is the focal point of the oppression of women.

This view is difficult to sustain because there is so much conflicting evidence – and what evidence there is is necessarily incomplete: an unknown number of violent sexual attacks on women go unreported. The Williams Report points out that the evidence linking porn and violence is of three types:

(i) anecdotal: the listing of cases of famous rapists who have 'used' pornographic magazines;

(ii)   evidence from psychological experiments;

(iii) the analysis of the correlation between the statistics on the availability of porn and the incidence of violent crimes against women.

Many radical feminists argue that there is evidence in favour of the causal thesis from all three sources. Let us look first at anecdotal evidence. It is said that both the Moors murderers and the Cambridge rapist in the UK regularly used porn magazines. Perhaps this is true, but there are also rapists who have not used porn. Anthony Burgess quotes the case of a multiple child murderer who was haunted by the Abraham–Isaac episode in the Old Testament.[54] A recent book, *Why Men Rape*,[55] documents the case histories of seven rapists. All came from difficult, disturbed backgrounds; all were insecure about sex and their masculinity (some did not think of themselves as 'proper' men), but not all of them had used porn magazines. Clearly, not every rapist has used porn magazines.

What about the second sort of evidence in favour of the causal thesis? There are conflicting reports from psychologists here. Some suggest that exposure to sexual material is cathartic, that it reduces violent activity. This notion was used by liberals in Denmark in arguing for a relaxation of the laws against prostitution. According to the catharsis model, symbolic systems including pornography allow men to release their aggression in harmless ways; they serve to sublimate the tabooed wishes they reveal. After the relaxation of Danish laws on pornography, Burt Kutchinsky found that with the increased availability of pornography there was a marked decline in the number of sexual offences.[56] His findings are dubious, however. Kutchinsky did not list rape as a separate sexual offence and so there is no knowing whether it decreased. In addition, some sexual offences were decriminalized in Denmark in the period between the liberalization of the porn laws and Kutchinsky's study, which would account for the decrease in the number of offences. And researchers have questioned the assumption underlining the catharsis model. McCormack points out that biases include 'the use of (mainly) male subjects, a logic dictated by a notion that for any theory of aggression or sexuality, men are the active group, men have the responsibility, and men confront the consequences of their own behaviour.'[57]

Similar objections have also been brought against other studies which support the 'porn as catharsis' view. But the evidence on the other side seems inconclusive too. For instance, research conducted by Seymour Fishback and Neal Malamuth uses an initiation model.[58] They found that college men who had viewed porn which connected sex with violence tended to be more sexually aroused by the idea of rape and less sympathetic to the victims than a control group who had not. But this study begs the question in favour of that form of pornography (a minority type, as we have seen) that connects sex with violence.

In another study, college students read two versions of a story from *Penthouse*. One group read a violent version, the other a non-violent one. They were then given a story about rape to read in which the 'terrified victim' was not aroused. The males who had read the violent story were more sexually aroused by the account of rape than the others. But the same criticism applies in the case of this study; it is not conclusive.

Finally, let us look at the analysis of trends. Some feminists claim that a greater number of rapes were committed in Britain between the years 1964 and 1972 than previously, and that this is positively correlated with an increase in the amount of readily available violent porn. Immediately we confront a problem of interpretation of the term 'violent'. Is the material in *Playboy* and other soft-core magazines seen here as violent? Between 1972 and 1979, there was an increase in the amount of British-based pornographic material with explicit sexual content, which included whippings, beatings, and so on.[59] But there was also during that period a reduction in the amount of hard-core violent porn imported. Additionally, though the number of rapes did increase during these years, all violent indictable offences increased by the same rate. So it looks, therefore, as though the cause of the increase lies outside porn. The causal connection is not proven.

I have looked at two arguments for the claim that male porn is the major agent expressing male power – one being that porn is itself a form of violence against women, and the other that porn causes violence against women. Both of these arguments have been found wanting.

Porn as 'the Graphic Depiction of Women as Vile Whores'

Dworkin goes right to the root of the word 'pornography' in her characterization of porn as 'the graphic depiction of women as vile whores.'[60] Men, she argues, 'created the group, the type, the concept, the epithet, the insult, the industry, the trace, the community, the reality of women as whores.' Here we have Dworkin at her powerful, rhetorical best. But once again, she misleads. First, she conflates two aspects of women's subordination: the actual violence to which women may be subjected in their homes or on the streets, and the imagery of pornography. Dworkin says 'the force depicted in pornography is objective and real because force is so often used against women.'[61] But the fact that force is so used against women does not make that in pornography 'objective and real'.

Secondly, Dworkin – through her overly literal rendering of the relation between porn and life – surely simplifies both the role of the prostitute and the meaning of sexual domination. The women who became harlots in order to survive in ancient Greece were in a very different position, socially and culturally, from those who took up the profession in order to serve soldiers in Vietnam. The men who go to prostitutes after having unwillingly suffered the horrors of the battlefield did not 'create the group, the type, the concept, the epithet, the insult, the industry, the trade, the commodity, the reality of women as whores'. More importantly for the definition of pornography, the poverty-stricken women whom soldiers of the Second World War visited in, say, Portsmouth, were vastly different in appearance, role and expectation from those portrayed in the blue movies shown to soldiers on their way to the Falklands War. Real prostitutes and the images of femininity in *Playboy* are quite different. Indeed, many a woman, forced by economic necessity to sell her body for the means of survival, would probably envy the attractive, relaxed personalities on the pages of *Penthouse* or on Page 3 of *The Sun*. The latter women are able, though being represented as fantasy objects, to present themselves as capable of enjoying sexual activity. Prostitutes do not necessarily appear to others in the same light.

Certainly, women are presented in some pornography as whores. In *My Secret Life*, a piece of Victorian pornography, the men chase after 'demireps, sluts and strumpets'. And many of the women the Marquis de Sade encountered sexually were prostitutes. Porn's representation of women as harlots, as women who have shamed themselves and stepped outside the limits of accepted culture and morality, serves to exonerate the men using the porn. It is the women who are made to be beyond morality, the women who are supposed to incite the men to debase and humiliate themselves.

As in the Garden of Eden, it is 'woman' – woman then beguiled by the serpent, now having transgressed the bounds of acceptable morality – who lures the men into her evil, dirty ways. But to suggest, as Dworkin does, an equation between the pornography of Christian culture, the pornography which absolves itself from shame by representing the women as having already sinned beyond all redemption, with *all* pornography – including recent blue movies and *Playboy* today – is surely to mislead. In our western, 'sexually liberated' world, our post-Freudian, post-Reichean culture, which allows sex scenes on television and nudity on Brighton beach, there is no need for women in pornography to be seen as whores. And surely they are not. Dworkin, perhaps, is too much of a Christian herself in her thinking about the subject.

In her literal characterization of porn, Dworkin sometimes forgets that pornography is a representation of fantasy. In her overwhelming desire to denigrate pornography, she ends up with a view of women in porn which is both inaccurate and which plays into the hands of her opponents by presenting whores as objects of condemnation. She says: 'in the male system, women are sex; sex is the whore.' Both are exaggerations. Not only do men not wear their dominance openly for all to see, but the majority of women are not, even in patriarchal cultures, either just 'sex' or just 'whores'. We are often exploited, oppressed and downtrodden – but we are not prostitutes.

Conclusion

I have argued, against Dworkin, that the pornography that is most widely disseminated today, both in the USA and Britain, does not involve the representation of violence against women. Nor is she correct in arguing that the subordination of women is equivalent to violence located in the penis, and perpetrated by men. Porn is not, I concluded, the paradigm case of the exercise of violent male sexuality.

I then discussed and criticized the claim made by other feminists that while porn may not itself constitute violence against women, it none the less causes it. I suggested here that the evidence for this claim is inconclusive. The focus on pornography as the centre of women's oppression is therefore wrong.

6
Dworkin: The Self

In Dworkin's recent book *Intercourse*, the views that are only implicit in her earlier work become explicit and graphic: 'intercourse and women's inequality are like Siamese twins, always in the same place at the same time, pissing in the same pot.'[1]

'Men have the power of naming'; 'Men have the power of self.' Women lack power. Men have; women lack. Men are; women are not. There are, I will argue here, deeper problems with Dworkin's thinking than any I outlined in the previous chapter. Dworkin has not completely left the individualist perspective behind.

First of all, compare Dworkin with Nietzsche. Dworkin admires Joan of Arc. Joan of Arc has an 'active self-determined integrity – existential independence'; Nietzsche's 'higher human beings' act out of an urge for 'self-affirmation'. 'Higher' types act, according to Nietzsche, not out of care, concern, or even duty, but out of self aggrandisement: a kind of superior self-knowledge of someone who is certain of where his or her true interests lie. 'The man who would not belong in the mass needs only to cease being comfortable with himself; he should follow his conscience which shouts at him: "Be yourself! You are not really all you do, think, or desire now".'[2] In Nietzsche's *The Gay Science*, giving 'style to one's character' is shown to be a sign of power.[3] In a similar vein, Dworkin says of Joan of Arc's virginity (symbolizing her power, independence and resistance to patriarchal values) that it is 'an existential independence, affirmed in choice and faith from minute to minute; not a retreat from life but an active engagement with it; dangerous and confrontational because it repudiated rather than endorsed male power over women.'[4] Nietzsche again: 'the man who has become free spurns the contemptible sort of well-being dreamed of by shopkeepers, Christians, cows, women, Englishmen and other democrats.'[5] Joan of Arc's virginity, says Dworkin, 'was an essential element of her virility', her autonomy, her rebellious and intransigent self-definition. Virginity was freedom from the real meaning of being female; it was not just another style of being female.'[6] Dworkin might almost have said that Joan 'spurned the contemptible sort of thing dreamed of by shopkeepers.' 'Being female', she says 'meant tiny boundaries and degraded possibilities; social inferiority and sexual subordination, obedience to men; surrender to male force or violence.'[7] Joan of Arc, by contrast, becomes strong, brave, masterful and proud, like Nietzsche's higher types.

Nietzsche was sceptical of virtue, concern and care of humanitarian qualities: 'Here everyone helps everyone else, here everyone is to a certain degree an invalid and everyone a nurse. This is then called virtue ...'[8] Christian virtues, Nietzsche believed, took the side of everything that was weak and base. They led to cowardice, they were the values of the downtrodden; they expressed 'the resentment (*ressentiment*)[9] of those who are denied the real reaction, that of the deed'.[10] They represented 'the *great* danger to mankind'.[11] The noble man – Socrates before his judges, Socrates in prison, Socrates meeting death, Socrates being powerful – 'shakes off with a *single* shrug many vermin that cut deep into others.'[12] (italics in original). Dworkin shares Nietzsche's view of Christian values: she admires virtue 'before the Christians got hold of it', when it meant 'brave' and 'valiant'.

Nietzsche is critical of those who are content to remain 'ordinary', those who 'demand nothing special of themselves, but for whom to live is to be every moment what they already are, without imposing on themselves any effort towards perfection; mere buoys that float on the waves.'[13] The 'select man', by contrast, 'is not the petulant person who thinks himself superior to the rest, but the man who demands more of himself than the rest ...'[14] For Dworkin, too, most women 'lack self'; only exceptional women transcend this lack. Joan of Arc's virginity, for instance, was 'an active element of self-determined integrity, an existential independence'.[15]

Nietzsche's critique is directed towards certain types (and groups) of people, Dworkin's towards patriarchal culture and its effects on women. Yet Dworkin comes dangerously close to criticizing women themselves, who fail (as most of us do) to live up to her Nietzschean standards of self-affirmation and self-mastery. Not far behind the description of Joan of Arc's 'contempt for the women who followed the soldiers as consorts or prostitutes' is Dworkin's contempt for such people. Behind the assertion that Joan had 'real and deep antipathies toward loose women' is Dworkin's antipathy towards them. Both Nietzsche and Dworkin are sceptical of the values associated with humanitarianism; care, sympathy and concern for others. Like Nietzsche, Dworkin denigrates Christian values. She associates them with women's oppression. Her contempt for Lucy, one of the virgins in the story of *Dracula*, is thinly disguised: 'She has no ambition, no substance, except that she is a female in the best sense.' Being a female 'in the best sense' for Dworkin means being 'compliant, ignorant, a virgin picking a husband'.[16] In her book *Right-wing Women*, Dworkin extends her contempt to ordinary women of today. The contemporary anti-feminist Marabel Morgan, she says, 'writes an awful, silly, terrible book in which she claims that women must exist for their husbands ...'[17]

But, as others have suggested,[18] there is no reason why the qualities traditionally associated with femininity should not be seen as sources of strength rather than weakness. There is no necessary connection between 'other-directed' concerns and subordination. Indeed, in her focus on the Nietzschean value of self-affirmation, Dworkin is embracing those aspects of the individualist tradition we rejected in Chapter 3. She dislikes dependency and need, and admires the strength and individual quest for freedom epitomized by (her portrait of) Joan of Arc. Thus she is closer to Bernard Williams et al. than it appears. Dworkin's 'ideal' women are very like the liberal individualist. They are not motivated by the collectivist values of care and concern for others, but by self-concern and a remarkable self-sufficiency.

Dworkin's critical attitude towards ordinary women is not peculiar to her as a feminist. Simone de Beauvoir's *The Second Sex*[19] evinced repugnance for the 'feminine' activities of childbearing and rearing. De Beauvoir viewed women who spent their time caring for others – notably their children – as trapped in 'immanence', as not really fully human, as having failed in any attempt at self-mastery. Intellectual women like herself, who refuse marriage, childbearing and caring, are the most likely of any women to transcend the role of 'the other', a position in which the majority of women are condemned to remain. For De Beauvoir, as with Dworkin, 'liberation' is achieved by self-mastery; while the feminine woman 'makes herself prey', the 'emancipated woman' 'wants to be active, a taker, and refuses the passivity men mean to impose on her.'[20] Just as Dworkin's Joan of Arc becomes a man, De Beauvoir's 'emancipated woman' accepts masculine values.[21] In order to be emancipated, De Beauvoir's woman must 'actively demand her sovereignty'; she must 'choose strength' and not weakness. But perhaps the most critical feminist picture of ordinary women and their domination by patriarchal conditioning is that given by Mary Daly. In her *Gyn/Ecology*[22], Daly describes women variously as 'moronised', 'robotised', 'lobotomised' and 'fembots' (a word she uses to mean 'like a feminine robot').

A number of feminists have criticized Dworkin, De Beauvoir, Daly and others for being over-general. Judith Okely, for instance, in her book *Simone de Beauvoir*,[23] criticizes de Beauvoir for failing to recognize that there are counter-examples to many of her generalizations about 'ordinary' women and to the myths of femininity. She suggests that many of de Beauvoir's general claims are applicable only to the very limited range of women she happened to encounter. De Beauvoir, according to Okely, presents 'an anthropological field study of Parisian cafe life in the thirties and forties, but without the anthropological theory and focus.'[24] 'Ordinary' women, in other words, are not as 'ordinary' as de Beauvoir makes out. There are many differences among them.

Lynn Segal offers a similar argument in her book *Is the Future Female?*[25] In a fashion that is reminiscent of Louis Althusser's denunciation of a range of thinkers from Descartes to Hegel through to the early Marx as 'empiricist', she labels the writings of Dale Spender, Mary Daly, Andrea Dworkin, Adrienne Rich, and the French feminists Julia Kristeva and Luce Irigaray, as 'essentialist'. These writers, according to Segal, make improper generalizations about spirituality, biology, language and the unconscious of women. These generalizations fail to give credence either to change in women's lives, or to the material, social, economic, racial and class differences among them. Essentialist feminism, she believes, downplays collective political struggle 'in favour of an alternative emphasis on cleaning our heads of "male ideas" or "male values".'[26] Segal contrasts the 'essentialist' project of much contemporary feminism, 'which stresses basic differences between men and women, and asserts the moral and spiritual superiority of female experience, values, character and culture ...' with a feminism which

> stresses the social and economic disadvantages of women and seeks to change and improve women's immediate circumstances, not just in the area of paid work and family life, but by providing funding for women's cultural projects, including women's safety in the streets or meeting the special needs of particular groups of women.[27]

I do not agree with Okely and Segal. I found Althusser's grouping of Hegel and Descartes peculiar because it downplayed the significant differences between these philosophers and I have a similar reservation about Segal's use of the label 'essentialist'. Luce Irigaray's mystical, psychoanalytical reading of 'woman's imaginary' is about as different from Andrea Dworkin's focus on violence against women as chalk is from cheese. And we need these theoretical works. Only if studies like Cynthia Cockburn's[28] (of the exclusion of women from print workers' work practices) are supplemented by theoretical analysis of class, race and gender will they have their intended impact. Without a theoretical underpinning the detailed studies would be just that, and would have no general import.

Dworkin and the Self

My reservations about Dworkin in particular, but also about de Beauvoir and Daly, are different. Dworkin writes as though liberation and self-mastery were a matter of personal choice: Joan of Arc, Mary Daly and Andrea Dworkin have perhaps all made the leap into virginity and away from the 'chattel' and 'object' status of women. But most women could be said, on Dworkin's thinking, to be in 'bad faith' about their own radical capacities; they deny their freedom and 'self-mastery' through being immersed in 'immanence'.

De Beauvoir drew on Hegel's analysis of the master and slave in formulating her view of the relation between the self and the other in interpersonal relations. (See Chapter 10 for further discussion of Hegel.) Every individual is engaged in a potentially dangerous struggle with other people in the assertion of freedom. Dworkin, too, sees life as a matter of struggle: violence, power, self-mastery (mastery over others too) are her favourite terms of art; care, love and sympathy are terms she rarely uses.

This picture of people – of women – as able to liberate themselves through radical choice, through mastery of themselves and others, ignores those aspects of life for which individuals are not responsible. Dworkin's individualist focus belittles collective responsibility. Improving women's conditions at work, gaining rights to childcare and abortion, introducing paternity leave and the need for fathers to care for children, are all ends achieved by collective action, and not by individual 'self-mastery' or choice. The woman who has five young children and survives on social security can achieve little change in her life by self-mastery. In D.H. Lawrence's *Sons and Lovers*,[29] Paul's mother is oppressed and constrained not so much by the sexual demands of her husband (he rarely makes them; why regard this as just one more 'male' ideological distortion of men's behaviour towards women?) as by her poverty, her four children and her illness. Individual choice may make very little difference to one's life when the external conditions are so bleak.

In fact most women would fare rather badly in Dworkin's hands. 'Men have self, and women must, by definition, lack it', she says. Women should transcend their object/chattel status by a vigorous act of will. But the majority of women fail ignominiously to meet this standard; they remain tools, possessions, chattels, objects, occupied territory in the hands of their male owners, possessors and occupiers. In Isaac Bashevis Singer's novel *Satan in Goray*, the character Rachel, Dworkin comments, 'had belonged to her father – her uncle ... a husband – and the *dybbuse*' (an evil spirit).[30] In *Dracula*, Lucy is 'compliant, ignorant';[31] Sophie, wife of Count Leo Tolstoy, is 'used by her husband as an object'.[32]

By referring to women as chattels, objects, as 'other', Dworkin is doing little to challenge a male-defined tradition of thinking about women. In much ancient Greek thought, women were regarded as being 'closer to nature' than men; Aristotle believed that women's souls were 'defective' in their ability to control the emotions. In the eighteenth century, Rousseau argued in *Emile* that women (personified through the character of Sophie) should be educated to be 'pleasing to men'. Kierkegaard and Sartre both saw woman as a 'being for another'; she had no existence or purpose in her own right. But there are many women who were not objects or chattels. Rosa Luxemburg, who was ugly, never made herself into an object; nor did Virginia Woolf or Emily Brontë. But it is not only 'transcendent' intellectuals who refuse the status of object. Working women during the Second World War, and the women described by the feminist historian Angela John[33] who have worked in the coal mines, are far from being chattels. Nor are the Chinese women who work in the fields, Asian women challenging suttee or the female supporters of the British miners' strike of 1984–5. Dworkin's view of women is misleading and denigrating.

For her, women are not only objects; they are self-deceiving, in thrall to patriarchal power. Lucy 'has no ambition, no substance'.[34] When she is finally discarded by Tolstoy, Sophie becomes a nervous wreck; 'unable to eat or sleep, crying uncontrollably, irritable, hostile, nervous'. Dworkin's women have a choice; they can be objects, or they can be deluded, dominated by false (patriarchally caused) desires. But this latter conception of the self – the view that there is a 'true' one (achievable by self-mastery) that underlies the patriarchal one – is again misleading. Descartes, we recall from previous chapters, construes the self as ultimately whole, unitary and undivided. Its essence is transparently clear to itself; it is a self-created 'ego'. Descartes believes in a 'false' self dominated by (illusory) sensory knowledge, and a 'true' self whose essence is thought. But Dworkin, too, believes that there are 'false' feminine selves, dominated by patriarchal conditioning, and 'true' selves, who have transcended this conditioning.

The view that there is a 'true' self underlying the illusory apparent one has come in for much recent criticism. Jacques Lacan,[35] for instance, has put forward the view that identity is inherently unstable: the unconscious prevents anyone from having a solid sense of self. Though most of us have a sense of ourselves as unitary and whole, this belief is illusory and derives from a stage in childhood development which he calls the 'Mirror Stage'. Prior to this, the child has drawn no distinction between subject and object between itself and the external world. Since it lacks the ability to symbolize the child before the Mirror Stage has no clear conscious sense of self. It is unconsciously unified, but it is at the same time merged with its 'mother' figure. But, if we imagine – and this is supposed to happen at about eighteen months – the child contemplating itself in a mirror, we can see how it begins to develop an integrated self-image: the child, who is still uncoordinated, sees a unified image of itself reflected in the mirror – a Gestalt. As Lacan puts it: 'We have only to understand the mirror stage as an *identification*, in the full sense that analysis gives to that term, namely the transformation that takes place in the subject when he assumes an image ...'[36] The sense of identity acquired by the child is illusory; actually she or he is still a mass of uncoordinated limbs. Furthermore, by inducing a split in the self between its 'reality', represented for Lacan by the unconscious, and its deceptive self-image, it has broken the previous unified, if unconscious, sense of self.

For Lacan, therefore, the Cartesian whole self is illusory. In fact, we are split and divided; there is a part of the self of which we are not conscious. But the Cartesian conception of the self, like Andrea Dworkin's, is also open to criticism from another perspective, that deriving from the contemporary French philosopher Jacques Derrida.[37] Beginning from the work of Ferdinand de Saussure, who has argued that linguistic and other signs gain their meaning not from their intrinsic properties, but by virtue of their differences from other signs, Derrida generalized this to any body of ideas or any text. There is no correct or true reading of a text: to assume that there is would be to claim that there is a definitive, clear-cut relationship between a piece of writing and its subject matter. And, Derrida avers, there is never such a relationship. Nor is there any such connection between the text and the thought of the author, or the truth about the world, and this is because no such privileged access is possible. Derrida argues the point by pointing to a series of examples, some of which appear to offer the strongest possible support for the claim. For instance, according to Descartes, the proposition 'I am; I exist' is necessarily true 'each time I pronounce it or conceive it in my mind.' But, Derrida would say, there is no pure access to the present in the way Descartes supposes. Each moment contains traces of the past and the future. An account of what is happening now, therefore, requires reference to other instances which are not present.

In the Derridean perspective, then, there is no access to the 'true' or the 'whole' self. Any attempt to gain entry to it will invariably contain traces of something outside it.

Yet while we cannot have full access to the true self, we cannot argue that there is no true self, or that any self is necessarily partially false. Any such argument is as dogmatic, as difficult to defend, as the view that it is opposing. Derrida himself would not attempt to claim that complete absence of a true self; it is an argument which is impossible to make, as one would have to refute all existing claims to have found the true self.

Instead of setting out to refute the claim that there is a 'true' and a 'false' self, I would rather express reservations about this claim *vis-à-vis* women. First of all, as we have seen with Dworkin, there is a tendency for a position relying on 'true' and 'false' women's selves to denigrate most women, who are condemned as leading false lives. Secondly, the perspective tends to make liberation from oppression an all-or-nothing matter: a woman is either free and manifesting her 'true' self or oppressed and dominated by patriarchal conditioning. In reality, most women are in a position somewhere between the two extremes. Most women have some liberated and some not-so-liberated characteristics. Thirdly, the perspective is over-cognitive; it emphasizes women rationally and wilfully coming to understand, accept and act in accordance with non-patriarchal values, while in practice women's lives contain much that is non-cognitive. Women cannot always rationalize away thoughts, feelings and other non-cognitive beliefs. Fourthly, fantasy plays a role in our lives that cuts across the 'true self' – 'false self' divide. For instance, while many woman today may have consciously, cognitively, rejected patriarchal conceptions of themselves, these values may none the less resurface in fantasy. Lynn Segal describes a common recurrent fantasy of being dominated by men – a domination for which in the real world these women have no desire at all.[38] Many feminist women, as we will see in a later chapter, are avid readers of romantic fiction, fiction that emphasizes values that, rationally, they would reject. Fifthly, and this is a matter to which I will return in a later chapter, the perspective gives insufficient weight to the resistance – both collective and individual – of many women to their oppression.

Finally, the view of Dworkin et al. attaches insufficient importance to conflicts and contradictions in women's lives. Jean Grimshaw, for instance, refers to Freud's description of obsessional neurosis, which

> is shown in the patient's being occupied with thoughts in which he is in fact not interested, in his being aware of impulses which appear very strange to him and in his being led to actions the performance of which give him no enjoyment, but which it is quite impossible for him to omit. The thoughts [obsessions] may be senseless in themselves, or merely a matter of indifference to the subject: often they are completely silly, and invariably they are the starting-point of a strenuous mental activity, which exhausts the patient and to which he only surrenders himself most unwillingly.[39]

Grimshaw writes that obsessional neurosis, for Freud, is 'characterised by the fact that the symptoms are not only debilitating, but are experienced as *alien* by the person; they do not seem "part" of him or her, and they seem discrepant with an everyday or normal sense of the self'.[40] In these cases, the self is split, as it were, against itself. The symptoms Freud is describing were not, as Grimshaw points out, thought by Freud to be uniquely characteristic of 'neurotic' patients; indeed, it is well known that Freud

> did not think much of the objection that neurotics form a special class of people, marked by an innate disposition that is 'degenerate', from whose childhood life we must not be allowed to infer anything about the childhood of other people. They cannot be sharply differentiated from normal people ...[41]

Even if we do not accept Freud's view of the matter, it is none the less true that most women experience conflicts and contradictions in their lives.

Ultimately, my major criticism of Dworkin's picture of the self is that it tends to denigrate the real experiences, conflicts and fantasies of most women and to idealize 'liberated' women. Because of her necessary attachment to radically different sets of values, the feminist today is even more likely than other women to experience conflicts in her identity. The 'emancipated' woman whose liberated self rejects marriage, subservience to men, speaking 'less' than men, etc., may, since she is living in a world which applauds them, admire men in fantasy. Women workers during the Second World War were likely to feel guilty about the children they had left behind. Margaret Thatcher, the strong, independent, archetypically masculine woman is also the strongest defender of women's role in the home, and she is, perhaps, strong and masculine enough for the commitment to the two sets of values not to be in conflict. Dworkin's view of the self, overall, is a liberal individualist one: her self is atomized, whole and unitary; she downplays the values of care for others and of dependence upon them; and she denigrates these conflicts in a woman's sense of her self.

A contrasting image of the self to that of Dworkin is a fragmented one, a self that is subject to conflicting, even contradictory, desires. I would like to illustrate this conception of the self by looking at the character of Sue in Thomas Hardy's novel, *Jude the Obscure*.[42] In some ways, as we will see, Sue is the epitome of a woman on the way to becoming a feminist.

Sue, the Divided Self

Hardy's story runs like this: Jude, a mason and an aspiring intellectual, leaves a disastrous marriage to Arabella (a woman who is given much less prominence in the book than Sue) to seek fame and fortune in 'Christminster', a city modelled on Oxford. He meets his cousin Sue and begins a complicated, difficult and lengthy platonic relationship with her that dominates both their lives. Partly to spite Jude for his marriage to Arabella, Sue marries Phillotson, a schoolteacher (she is a teacher herself) who is much older than she, and who, though she likes and respects him, physically repels her. She eventually leaves him and returns to live with Jude; they care for Jude and Arabella's child, whose life's misfortunes have made him morose and old for his years, and whom they call 'Father Time'. They also have two children of their own.

One day, their fortunes at a particularly low ebb, Sue and Jude search for lodgings. They find it difficult to persuade a landlady to take them in. Eventually, Sue and the children move in to one room and Jude goes off to find somewhere cheaper for himself. After a conversation between Sue and Father Time, in which she expresses the view that it would have been easier for Sue and Jude without the children, she returns to her room to find all three children hanged.

After this tragedy, Jude attempts to continue life as before, but Sue apparently undergoes a personality change. From being an in-dependent, intellectual and unconventional (although always vacillating) woman, she becomes subservient and conventional. She returns to Phillotson.

We can see Sue as the epitome of a woman who is on her way to becoming a feminist. Psychologically, she is like the typical feminist of the 1970s or 1980s in Europe or America. Although her conflicts are more marked than they would be today, they are, none the less, similar. Yet, even early this century, self-proclaimed feminists were railing against Hardy for not making Sue a 'whole self'. One 'experienced reviewer'[43] from Germany informed Hardy (after the novel had been serialized in a German magazine early this century) that Sue Bridehead was

> the first delineation in fiction of the woman who was coming into notice in her thousands every year – the woman of the feminist movement – the slight, pale 'bachelor' girl – the intellectualised emancipated bundle of nerves that modern conditions were producing, mainly in cities as yet; who does not recognise the necessity for most of her sex to follow marriage as a profession, and boast themselves as superior people because they are licensed to be loved on the premises.

The reviewer then went on to regret that the portrait of Sue had been drawn by a man, and not by a woman, who would never have allowed her to break down in the end.

This is a complete failure to see the complexities in Sue's character. For, I shall argue, Sue's 'breaking down' (as the critic puts it) is crucial to her sense of herself as a woman, a feminist and a radical. Indeed, I would argue (and perhaps it is only because I am a woman, and would call myself a feminist, that I can argue this way) that the fact that the character of Sue was drawn by a man is not only *not* detrimental to her nature as a complex woman, but indeed has resulted in a picture that more closely approximates the real thing – the intellectual, feminist woman of today or of the 1890s – than the reviewer's notion of the feminist woman.

Can we make the case that Sue is a feminist? On the surface it is doubtful. We are never given so much as a glimpse into her thoughts as we constantly are with Jude's and even Phillotson's. Other than the veiled remarks about her made by Jude's aunt, and her own fragmentary verbal reminiscences, we know very little about her past, although we know plenty about Jude's. We might be led to think that Sue is the very antithesis of a feminist when we read Jude's unsympathetic remark about Sue towards the end of the novel: 'What I can't understand in you is your extraordinary blindness now to your old logic. Is it peculiar to you, or is it common to women? Is a woman a thinking unit at all, or a fraction always wanting its integer?' Or this, in a critical commentary on Jude '[Jude's] experiences [have] enlarged his view of life ... The opposite happens to Sue. The girl whose intellect scintillated like a star cannot hang on to her independence of mind when tragedy strikes her, and she goes back to the husband whom she should never have married ...'[44]. Jude's remark about Sue can be read as a criticism of women: they are irrational, illogical, unthinking beings. In a way that is reminiscent of Luce Irigaray's association of visual imagery with masculinity (see Chapter 3), Sue is 'blind' to her old logic. As a woman, her mental vision has gone, and she is unable to 'see' reason. And yet a woman may be a fraction always wanting its integer: thus a woman becomes incomplete, a fragment.

These quotes suggest that women are presented in the novel in a negative light, as props for the principal male characters. And yet there is plenty of evidence to the contrary in the text. It is not only the male characters whose internal thoughts are presented. Ironically, perhaps we are given insight into Arabella's inner world. Indeed we learn more about Arabella's background than we do about Jude's. Does this not suggest that Sue is deliberately left enigmatic? As for the critic's view, I think, and I will argue this in a moment, that this is a distortion of the text.

There are ways in which Sue is obviously a feminist, at least one of the 1890s. She is educated; she spends much of her time teaching. She uses her education to express feminist views; she criticizes marriage laws as enslaving, and expresses the view that 'in a proper state of society the father of a woman's child' [is] a private matter of hers.'[45] Indeed it is Sue, and not Jude or Phillotson, who quotes one of the most radical theorists of the period on women's liberation, J.S. Mill. Sue is critical of the 'tyranny of prevailing opinion and feeling'; she thinks that human happiness is more important than institutions like marriage, for instance. Sue quotes from Mill when she wants to leave Phillotson:

"She or he who lets the world, or his own portion of it, choose his plan of life for him, has no need of any other faculty than the ape-like one of imitation." It is Mill's words those are. I have been reading them up. Why can't you act on them. I wish to always.'

'What do I care about Mill,' moaned he [Phillotson]. 'I only want to lead a quiet life.' [46]

The passage Sue quotes comes from the section 'On Liberty' in *Individuality*, and the obvious point that Mill is making is that people should be individuals: they should choose their own plan of life, and should not conform. But implicit in what Sue is groping towards is the idea that marriage – the world's choice – subordinates the woman more than the man, and she, the woman, therefore has to choose another course. This reading of Sue's meaning is also suggested by a later remark by Phillotson in which he says that he has 'out Sue'd Sue' in proposing that perhaps the 'women and children should be the unit without the man.'[47] Mill, after all, in *On the Subjection of Women*[48] describes the role of the wife in marriage as being rather like that of a slave.

Sue's remark metaphorically extends this notion of marriage as slavery. Slaves are denied their humanity; are said to become 'non-human and animal-like', human beings in form but lacking rationality, that distinctive feature of humanity. Sue implies that anyone who allows herself to be subjected to the 'world's' plan of life' effectively ceases to be a human being; she fails to give expression to her humanity. Thus Sue herself is both giving expression (a radical thing in itself) to the idea of marriage as 'enslaving' women and suggesting that both men and women must transcend their conditioning in order to be fully human. This view of hers prefigures the ideas of Simone de Beauvoir, for whom, as we have seen, women must transcend their conditioning, and indeed their bodies, in order to realize fully their true potential as human beings.

So there is a sense in which Sue is a feminist. She can certainly be read as the nineteenth-century counterpart of the twentieth-century feminist; her radicalism leads to a conflict at the very core of her being. Sue and Jude are ostracized for their beliefs, and they are punished by their children in the most dreadful way. For Sue, however, the experience leads to a conflict of identity in a way that it does not for Jude, and this, I believe, is because she is a woman. Sue believes, with Mill, that everyone should be free to choose to live as they wish, and yet, because she is a woman, she cannot express her view, as Jude does, in the pub or to the assembled multitudes in Christminster. No woman, whatever her class or race, would have been able to express views of any kind openly, dissenting or otherwise. As a woman, she does not have the opportunity to present even a facade of certainty in public, as Jude does to a much greater extent.

The critic who derided Sue for her behaviour at the end of the book and upheld Jude as steadfast, and the early feminist writer who claimed that a woman would not have allowed Sue to alter as she did, are surely missing something. As a woman, Sue would have been closer to their children than Jude; she bore two of them, and she spends more time looking after all three than Jude, who is out at work for much of the day. That, and her adult-level conversation with 'Father Time' the night before the children's deaths, suggests that she will feel their deaths and blame herself more deeply than Jude. Thus, she has to come to terms, somehow or other, with their death. Continuing in her previous way of life – living moderately happily with Jude, though with many difficulties would have been impossible for her because it would have been a constant reminder of her loss and guilt. She must try to forget the loss and assuage her guilt; the only way open to her is to return to the husband she does not love. Phillotson is clearly physically repugnant to her, so returning to him represents for her both a means of self-punishment and a way of moving away from her previous existence. There is no other way of performing these two tasks; contemporary solutions – to travel far away or to live alone – are closed to her. In addition, there are the complexities of Sue's past. We are given to believe that part of the reason for her marriage to Phillotson was to spite Jude for his marriage to Arabella. This, no doubt, was not all of it – Phillotson had proposed to her, he would provide for her, and marriage gave her a kind of respectability, to the attractions of which she is unlikely to have been immune. Jude was unavailable; no one else was on the horizon; marriage to Phillotson enabled her to continue teaching, which she clearly enjoyed. Her guilt on leaving him was not only to do with a lingering respect for the conventions – although that is bound to have been there: how many of us can easily, and with no qualms or doubts, give up the received mode of behaviour? – but it is also a feeling that she had been ungrateful for all that he had done for her. The change in her at the end is not so great, given all this, and given, too, that throughout her time with Jude she preserves an attachment to Phillotson as a friend and mentor. Does she not visit Phillotson when he is ill, and show concern about him? Thus, there is not so much a radical change in character at the end of the book (as even Jude himself thinks there is) as a constant hesitation, vacillation, fragmentation at the very core of her being that is characteristic of women in general, and of feminist women in particular.

The reading I have offered of Hardy's presentation of the character Sue makes her out to be, as a fragmented self, typical of many women, both of today and of the late-nineteenth century. Indeed, as we will see later, we find the same sort of fragmentation expressed in recent romantic fiction. In many a romantic novel, for instance, the heroines are presented as people who swing rapidly from being independent, autonomous beings to being dutiful, passive lovers. Many a heroine of a 1980s novel who starts out as a representative of 1980s progressivism becomes a dutiful wife.

This interpretation of Sue suggests an alternative to Dworkin's virginal Joan of Arc. Instead of emphasizing the masculine, individualist qualities of self-mastery, power and domination (of self or others), it emphasizes an attachment to 'feminine' values of care, sympathy and concern, *and* to the 'masculine' ones of independence and strength. But it also points to conflict in the woman's sense of self: as for many women, there is no clear-cut set of wants and interests that Sue knows she has and can set out to fulfil. Rather, she is constantly torn between her would-be conception of herself as free and independent, and a desire, despite herself, to continue fulfilling the role of the married woman, in thrall to her men.

Conclusion

In this chapter, I have examined the Nietzschean elements in Dworkin's work and expressed reservations about the conception of the self that underlies it. The argument suggests that Dworkin is not as far removed as she would no doubt like to be from the individualist perspective. Her view of the self, and of the 'liberated' woman, with its emphasis on the 'masculine' values of self-mastery and power, and with its focus on the true self having interests that are self-evident to it, is not far from the rational, whole individual of the Williams Report. Despite Dworkin's recognition that due weight must be given to the gender of the people depicted in the pornographic magazines, she does not, in the end, properly distance herself from the individualist perspective. Indeed, she underplays collectivities other than those of gender, namely class and race.

7

The Freudian Griffin

Another influential contemporary radical feminist writer on pornography is Susan Griffin. For her, 'pornography is an expression ... of a fear of bodily knowledge, and a desire to silence eros.'[1] 'The bodies of women in pornography, mastered, bound, silenced, beaten and even murdered', she writes in *Pornography and Silence*,

> are symbols for natural feeling and the power of nature, which the pornographic mind hates and fears ... We will come to see that 'the woman' in pornography, like 'the Jew' in anti-Semitism and 'the black' in racism, is simply a lost part of the soul, that region of being the pornographic or racist mind would forget and deny. And finally, we shall see that to have knowledge of this forbidden part of the soul is to have eros.[2]

I will argue that Griffin's analysis falls foul of a different set of difficulties from those encountered by Dworkin, but that she, like Dworkin, although for different reasons, has failed to extricate herself from the individualist perspective.

By means of a suggestive series of examples, from Don Juan to the *femme fatale*, from de Sade to Marilyn Monroe, Griffin argues that what is characteristic of porn is the absence of Eros. In pornographic culture 'there is no tenderness.' Don Juan knows none of the vulnerability of love. '[He] makes love without falling in love. The whole *oeuvre* of the Marquis de Sade', Griffin claims, 'can be taken as an obsessive ridicule of eros.'[3]

Griffin argues that pornography expresses a hatred born out of fear of the body, nature, the feminine, women and, primarily, of feeling. 'The pornographic mind seeks revenge on feeling.'[4] The 'darkness' of the female, she suggests, which expresses a side of man of which he is afraid, and which he wishes to control, is threatening. Therefore women must be subdued, silenced, mastered. The man, personified as 'the pornographic mind' calls himself 'culture', she says, and separates himself from nature and women. The metaphysics of Christianity and of porn, she suggests, are the same. Both seek to subdue and control nature and feeling.

Pornography, she claims, 'destroys feeling';[5] the novel *Justine*, for example, involves 'the death of the heart'.[6] However, pornography does not exclude all feeling, for typically it arouses desire, a particularly strong feeling. It produces sexual desire, and the wish to dominate. But it also expresses these desires in relation to the self: the pornographer projects onto a fantasy image of a woman – whether she is Marilyn Monroe, Justine, or the heroines of novels such as *Captive Virgin*, *Behind the Green Door*, and *Fatherly Love* – his own fear and hatred of his bodily desire. According to Griffin, pornography therefore expresses the pornographer's desire for self-mastery, self-control – his desire to control his natural, sensual, animal side. If Griffin's 'pornographic imagination' excludes feeling, it is not these feelings. Rather, it is the kind of feelings that have sometimes been described as the 'feminine' feelings of care, concern and helplessness. Two tales, the Greek tragedy *Iphigenia* and de Sade's *Justine*, tell the story of civilization's sacrifice of an innocent and vulnerable young woman. Yet *Iphigenia*, Griffin tells us, is not pornography. What separates it from *Justine* is feeling:

> To watch Agamemnon send his daughter to death is almost unbearable. We are outraged. We hope. With Clytemnestra we pray and plead for her life. And when she dies, we weep, as if one we loved, or a part of ourselves, were lost. But one never weeps as a witness to pornography. No death in pornography touches us with sorrow. Justine's suffering fails to move us. We cannot imagine loving Justine, and we let her die with no protest, because as we enter the mind of the Marquis de Sade, our hearts are silenced.[7]

Feelings

Griffin says that pornography involves the death of feeling. But one cannot help recalling those women who, according to Williams et al., were 'outraged' by pornography. Thus porn sometimes gives rise to one of the feelings we experience on reading *Iphigenia*. And one wonders whether everyone would respond to *Justine* in the fashion Griffin describes. If they do, might it not have something to do with de Sade's dry, eighteenth-century rationalist prose, rather than with pornography's success in silencing feeling? I doubt whether many would agree that D.H. Lawrence's *Lady*

Chatterley's Lover 'silenced' feeling, in Griffin's sense, in every reader, or that pornographic films about lesbian sex which are directed primarily towards men, do so in all women. The reservations I am expressing here have partly to do with the fact that pornography is produced in a particular social context and reactions to it vary depending on that context. As the feminist writer Marianne Valverde put it:

> When I give talks about pornography, I often bring with me a glossy photo showing a very young girl climbing on a large white couch. The girl is naked and one sees her from behind, with her bum figuring prominently in the middle of the picture. Now, if I tell people I found the picture in *Penthouse*, they'll agree that it is child pornography. But if I tell them that it is a picture I took of my niece, they tend to agree that it is not porn. And, when I finally tell them the truth, which is that I cut it out of *Cosmopolitan*, they scratch their heads.[8]

Valverde assumes that if she herself had taken the picture of her niece, then it would not be porn. What if she had taken it in order to sell it to *Penthouse*? Or if her father/husband/lover had used it as an image towards which to direct his masturbatory fantasies? It is said that copies of *National Geographic Magazine* were once bought in Britain for precisely this purpose. But part of Valverde's point is that 'our' reactions to porn depend on the nature of the porn, and on who 'we' are. If the porn is a copy of *National Geographic*, and 'we' are geography students in a geography class, then our reaction to it is no doubt very different from that of a group of older men, all experiencing problems in their 'sex' lives, watching a film about lesbian sex in Soho. Griffin is surely over-generalizing about 'our' reactions to certain representations and not to others when she claims that pornography silences feeling while 'art' does not. As Susanne Kappeler[9] (see Chapter 8) has argued, the distinction between 'porn' and 'art' is a very difficult one to sustain.

The qualities that pornography humiliates, denounces and silences are those that the individualist tradition also degrades. Pornography, in Griffin's view, silences the caring, humanitarian part of a person. 'The pornographer, like the Church father, hates and denies a part of himself.'[10] Pornography projects a one-sided image of a person as a 'mind' consumed by fear of the body and humanitarian feeling, and as wanting to master those aspects of himself. Thus, the perspective of Griffin's 'pornographic mind' is also, to some degree, the individualist viewpoint, the Nietzschean picture, and, dare we say it, that of Dworkin's 'strong' women. Like Griffin's pornographers, Dworkin's strong, independent women are contemptuous of humanitarian care and concern. Griffin's 'pornographic mind' is primarily the mind of the man projecting onto women his own fears of his body, but it is also, she says, the mind of Christianity. 'We might', she says, 'name the story of Jesus Christ as the origin of culture's torture of the body. All the elements of sado-masochistic ritual are present in the crucifixion of Christ. And the Christian religion itself labours to deny the body.'[11]

If porn and Christianity, as Griffin says, 'share the same metaphysics', so too does any other body of thought that seeks, as they both do, to 'silence' humanitarian feeling and to belittle the classically 'feminine' qualities of care and concern for others. Thus Griffin's pornographers 'share the same metaphysics' as Dworkin's strong, independent women. At the risk of being glib, it is worth pointing out that Dworkin is not a pornographer and neither was Christ. Griffin's juxtaposition of porn and Christianity defuses the peculiar wrongs that attach to pornography. The silencing of humanitarian feeling is quite a general phenomenon; it appears, after all, in Descartes' notion of 'man' as a 'rational animal'. But this is far removed from pornography. Only if we take Francis Bacon's image of knowledge involving a marital union between the rational (masculine) mind and the non-rational (female) nature, where the knowing mind seeks to control and dominate nature, do the two images come together. But this, on Griffin's premises – where marital union gives expression to feeling – would not be pornographic.

Projection

Griffin's idea is that the man, the exemplification of the 'pornographic mind', projects on to the woman his own fear and hatred of his body and his humanitarian feelings. She analyses this, Freudian fashion, as having to do with his fear, as a small boy, of his mother's power. 'Do we not discover this very mechanism of the mind to confuse one's own body with the body of one's mother in the pornographer's projection of his own denied self onto the objectified image of a woman?'[12] Often in pornography, Griffin notes, 'we find the image of a woman sucking a man's penis [which] is emblematic', she says, 'of another situation ... In the film *The Devil and Miss Jones*, for example, when the heroine is taught oral lovemaking, she begins to desire this act with an unrealistic avidity. She seeks this act as if her life depended on it. She becomes a nymphomaniac, almost maddened by her wanting. Her eyes take on a lurid and a frantic quality.'[13] This image, Griffin suggests, 'reminds the mind of another scene ... For it is the infant who so overwhelmingly needs the mother's breast at his mouth. The infant who thought he might die without this, who became frantic and maddened with desire, and it was his mother who had the power to withhold.'[14]

Griffin's idea that the man's projected feelings derive from a childhood sense of helplessness is described by the contemporary feminist psychologist Wendy Hollway. She claims that the man often projects on to the woman his own vulnerability and neediness. The man can then appear strong, in control, while the woman, who may not really be these things, becomes weak and needy. She quotes men who admit to being 'frightened of strong emotions', like Griffin's pornographers.[15] Hollway suggests that 'desire for the other (the man for the woman) is desire for the mother.' If he is in a sexual relationship, the man wants from that woman the total adoration he received from his mother. One character she describes, Jim, said that his lover, Wendy, pretended to like classical music as he did as a way of saying 'I love everything about you.' Hollway argues that the woman in a relationship with a man is often stronger and less vulnerable than the man, reflecting the fact that the mother has power over the child.

Hollway believes that in some sense the woman really does have power over the man, although the power she has in the private sphere is counterposed by the power of the man in the 'public' world of work. Griffin downplays any actual power the woman may have by focusing on the manifold attempts, through various systems of representation, made by the 'pornographic mind' to suppress and control that power. The repression of this power appears in the male representation of femininity, the body and feeling which is expressed, she says, in the image of the woman in the book *A Captive Virgin*, who feels delight when she is forcibly penetrated. It is shown in de Sade's *Justine* when a woman is abducted and raped by monks. But, Griffin suggests, feeling cannot be fully controlled, because the woman, who represents feeling, is alive and sometimes well. Thus, Griffin argues, the images in porn 'become increasingly violent' and often end in women's deaths. In Arctino's *Dialogue of the Life of a Married Woman*, 'a wife pretends to be near death so that she can commit adultery with the priest when she has called for her last confession.'[16] Death, in pornography, represents the death of feeling and virtue. The heroine of de Sade's *Philosophy in the Bedroom*, as she anticipates the arrival of a child to whom she is to teach this philosophy, promises: 'Be certain I'll spare nothing to prevent her, degrade her, demolish in her all her false ethical notions with which they may already have been able to dizzy her; in two lessons, I want to render her as criminal as am I ... as impious ... as debauched, as depraved.'[17]

Griffin is not the first to have linked sex and death. In *Beyond the Pleasure Principle*, Freud described 'the drive to inorganicism' as 'the most radical form of the pleasure principle.' None the less, we encounter a few problems with Griffin's analysis. First of all, if we look at Hegel's master–slave dialectic and its relevance for the analysis of porn, the slave, the woman, must not (always) die, for the master, the pornographer, needs her in order both to satisfy his desire and (on Griffin's analysis) to continue to project on to her his fears of his own emotion.

Secondly, as I argued earlier, there is plenty of porn that does not depict violent images of women. Moreover, the evidence showing that violence in porn is increasing is dubious. Most studies suggest that the amount of violence depicted rises at certain times and falls at others. One study carried out by psychologist Neil Malamuth concluded that the number of violent pictures in *Penthouse* dropped slightly from 1973 to 1975, and then increased sharply to the end of 1977. *Playboy*, by contrast, showed a dramatic increase in violent content from 1973 to 1975, then declined in 1976.

One must treat studies like this with a certain amount of scepticism; the female researcher in the above study, for instance, invariably found more violent images than her male counterpart. As Valverde puts it: 'the differences in perception were most apparent in their evaluation of cartoons, which often appeared as funny to the man and as violent to the woman.'[18] In the experimental report, however, the woman's perceptions were neutralized by being averaged with those of the male. None the less, whichever way one looks at the matter it is doubtful that one could prove an increase in the violent content of porn to confirm Griffin's conclusion that porn was 'becoming increasingly violent'. Griffin, no doubt, intends the metaphor to be just that, a metaphor, yet it must bear some relation to the actual content of pornographic magazines for it to carry any weight.

A second reservation about Griffin's metaphor concerns her Freudian focus on the little boy's relationship to his mother. The boy's hatred and fear of his humanitarian feelings and vulnerability arises, according to her Freudian perspective, out of his memory of his being in thrall to his mother's power. However, some of the most misogynistic men have not been cared for by their mothers. Jean Jacques Rousseau, for instance, who believed that women 'should be educated to be pleasing to men', was not brought up by his mother since she died in his infancy. It is highly unlikely that Aristotle, another misogynist, was brought up by his natural mother in a classically Freudian nuclear family. And it is notable that, of the twelve case studies documented in *Why Men Rape*,[19] almost all the rapists had difficult, disturbed backgrounds, with a mother who had very little power in the household. (Few of them, moreover, had much exposure to pornographic magazines.)

The Freudian Griffin might respond to this by saying that while it may be true that many men have not been brought up by their mothers, most of them will have been cared for by women. The Freudian view would therefore still hold. This is certainly true, but the critical point, I think, illustrates that Griffin's Freudian focus overemphasizes one side of the 'pornographic mind' at the expense of others. It illustrates that she is still an individualist.

Griffin's Freudian focus on the relationship between mother and child is 'individualistic' in this sense: it abstracts the mother–son relationship from the collectivities of family, class, race and, ultimately, from society. The little boy is not just that, he is the son of members of a particular class, race, and his upbringing was not just in 'the family', it was in a Bengali extended family in India, or an English middle-class 'nuclear' network, or a white Anglo-Saxon American collective into which he had been adopted from South America or a Jewish ghetto family in Eastern Europe. Each of these units is located in a variety of social and cultural settings. The membership of the little boy and his 'mother' of these radically disparate collectivities will influence his feelings towards her and her power. The power of third-world women working in the fields throughout multiple pregnancies cannot be precisely akin to that of the mother rearing her son in Britain in the 1950s under the influence of the texts of Dr Spock.

Griffin: 'the image of a woman sucking a man's penis ... with an unrealistic avidity ... reminds the mind of another scene ... for it is the infant who so overwhemingly needs his mother's breast at his mouth. The infant who thought he might die without this, who became frantic and maddened with desire, and it was his mother who had the power to withhold.' Does the bottle have the same power for those children who are bottle-fed? Does the father who wields the bottle possess the same power as the mother with her all-powerful breast? And what of the relationship of girl child to her mother: why does that between boy and mother depart so dramatically from the binding connection between little girl and her mother? Because Griffin abstracts a larger-than-life 'boy-mother' relationship from the collectivities of family, social setting and culture, she can ignore these other relationships that must inform and transform the general 'boy–mother' couple. And not just relationships, but cultural meanings attached, for example, to breastfeeding, must influence the 'power' of the breast. The power of mother and breast for the little boy is mitigated by breastfeeding being regarded, in many spheres, as an indication of a woman's inferiority: one writer describes how in the House of Commons in the early 1980s breastfeeding provoked 'sniggers from some men and covert hostility from some women members' who fear that in being associated with someone who is breastfeeding, they will be identified as "women" and therefore "out of place" in this male club.'[20]

A further aspect of Griffin's individualism is brought out if we look at another facet of pornography. Porn is big business. A major motivation for the production and dissemination of the most popular pornographic magazines is simply that they sell. During a six-month period in 1980, for instance, *Penthouse* grossed $8,556,075 in Canada alone (which is only one-tenth of world-wide sales); *Playboy* made $5,603,400. Berthe Milton's annual profits from the hard-core magazine *Private* 'could easily be in the region of $500,000'.[21] With money like this, the producers of porn are obviously going to do whatever they can to continue, and their motivation might have nothing whatsoever to do with fear of their mothers. Their unconscious motivation, indeed, might simply be greed. They might not even look at the magazines. Finally, feminist analysts of porn have to take stock of the fact that, for whatever reasons, women as well as men buy pornographic magazines. A Canadian survey carried out by the Ragley Commission showed that 'three out of five males and about one in three females stated that they had bought pornography at least once.'[22] Even if the women bought the magazines 'just to see what they were like', they are contributing to the high sales figures and the vast profits. Moreover, one of the 'porn barons', the owner of a West German porn chain, is a woman, Beate Uhse.[23] Feminist publicity – though we must be very careful here – might even have boosted their sales. The case of *Spycatcher*, banned in the UK in 1988 and topping the best-seller lists in the USA, illustrates the boost to sales given by publicity of any kind, and notably by attempts to ban or suppress a work.

The point I am making is this. Any exploration of the popularity of pornography must give proper credence to the multifaceted influences on an individual, and to the many roles any one individual takes on in society today. We are not just men and women; we are also members of classes and races. It is as members of the class of the very rich that the major shareholders of *Penthouse* derive pleasure from pornography. Even if the desire to sell millions of copies of the magazine derives from an unconscious wish to get back at their mothers, their present pleasures come mainly from the desire to make even greater profits, a desire which, as Karl Marx pointed out in *Das Capital*, can become an end in itself. The capitalist, he said, becomes 'capital personified'.[24] Similarly, the woman who buys a copy of *Penthouse*, unless she is very rich, is a member of the class from whose labours the capitalist profits. In this respect, and even though she might be offended by the magazine, she is just like her male counterpart who buys the magazine in order to give vent to his masturbatory fantasies.

With her aversion to the values of self-mastery and self-control, Griffin goes some way in her criticism of the individualist perspective. But she does not go far enough. A full rejection of its pre-suppositions must recognize that agents in the pornographic mind and in the pornographic production and consumption process are not just men and women. Whatever our gender, we are also members of classes and races, and this membership is part of the explanation for the popularity of pornography. The fact of class and gender contributes to explaining what is wrong with porn.

Conclusion

I have discussed Susan Griffin's 'pornographic mind'. I have argued that her Freudian focus on porn as the projection of men's fears and hatred of the body and of feeling misses out on one vital fact, namely, that pornography is big business. As producers of porn, men are not just, or even primarily, men; they are capitalists, governed by the desire for profit. And as consumers of porn, men and (sometimes) women are not just that, but are also members of the class on the fruits of whose labours the capitalist survives. A proper critique of the individualist perspective on porn must give credence to these facts.

8
Kappeler and Representation

A recent and beautifully written book by Susanne Kappeler extends the debate about pornography to 'representation' in general. 'The history of representation is the history of the male gender representing itself to itself – the power of naming is men's ... Culture, as we know it, is patriarchy's self-image.'[1]

Kappeler is keen to extricate herself from the individualist perspective. She attaches importance to 'attempt(s) to establish a connection between the individual victim and a class of potential victims.'[2] She begins her book by describing the murder of Thomas Kasire, a black Namibian farmworker, by two white men. For Thomas, she suggests, 'put "Justine", or "Emmanuelle" or "O" – the victim already designated by "reduced identity".'[3] Thus she metaphorically draws connections between the various groups of powerless 'victims' in society. The white male murderers, who photograph their despicable act as they carry it out, represent white men in general. The promise of her book is a focus on the collectives of gender, class and race. Unfortunately, this promise is not fulfilled.

On the surface Kappeler's book is very different from the radical feminist writing of Dworkin et al. Not for her is Dworkin's belief that pornography lies at the heart of male supremacy; nor does Kappeler focus on violent pornography to the exclusion of other forms. Yet, probing beneath the surface, we find that Dworkin and Kappeler are very close. Despite herself, and like Dworkin, Kappeler has not entirely left the individualist perspective..Both proceed by powerful rhetoric, metaphor and persuasion rather than by argument. And Kappeler shares with Dworkin a black and white view of male supremacy. Kappeler's conviction that men 'have the power of naming'[4] could have come directly from Dworkin. Like Dworkin, Kappeler believes that 'language is male.'[5]

These views, epitomized in Dale Spender's *Man Made Language*,[6] have been much criticized by feminists (see, for example, Segal, Grimshaw and Assiter). I have argued that if men and women speak different languages, and occupy different realities, then men's and women's worlds are incommensurable, and women cannot begin convincing men of the viability of their case.

Kappeler's position, moreover, is ambiguous, and this obscures the nature of her target. On the one hand, she suggests that feminists concerned about pornography should move away from a specific focus on *Playboy*, de Sade, blue movies, etc., to look more generally at representation. Drawing on examples from literature and art, she suggests that representation presupposes that men are subjects, the authors or the readers; women are the objects. Underlying any representational form is the image of the male as the viewer and the woman as the object of the viewing. 'We as women share in the cultural apprenticeship of perceiving the "beautiful" in certain ways, and these ways are indebted to the male perspective of the viewer.'[7] Kappeler quotes John Berger: 'Men look at women. Women watch themselves being looked at.'[8]

One of Kappeler's claims, therefore, is that representation in general, and not pornography, as one form of representation, should be the feminist target. But there is another view which becomes intertwined with this one, and which at times appears to be Kappeler's focus. This is that representation in general becomes pornography. Kappeler does not so much state this position as suggest it. She describes a 1984 article in the *Guardian Weekly*, entitled 'A Murder in Namibia'. The article is about a white farmer who had tortured and killed Thomas Kasire, a new black worker on his farm. There are, Kappeler says, three pictures accompanying the article, two of which are from the scene of the crime: one showing a close-up of the boy's head, bleeding, one ear half cut off, a heavy iron chain around his neck. 'The victim is forced to pose with a clenched fist (the SWAPO salute), while a friend of the murderer takes photos.'[9] Using a suggestive series of substitutions, 'a woman in the place of the black man', the white men in their respective positions, Kappeler says: 'the picture may remind us, or some of us, of pornography.'[10] Of course, to say that the picture reminds her of pornography is not at all the same as saying that it is pornography, but when this case is taken together with others, Kappeler's position becomes more explicit. For example, in her chapter 'Art and Porn', she argues that it is the conjuncture of the pornographic with the literary that gave D.M. Thomas's novel *The White Hotel* instant acclaim. In other words, a 'good' piece of artistic representation will combine the qualities of artistry and pornography.

A further example of the elision of representation with pornography occurs in the chapter 'Subjects, Objects, and Equal

Opportunities'. Kappeler uses Kant's analysis of 'the aesthetic' to describe the relation between the artist/reader and cultural product. According to Kant, delight in art involves 'disinterested' pleasure. 'The judgement of taste ... must involve a claim to validity for all men.'[11] Kappeler says: 'Might the disinterested aesthetic pleasure perchance be gendered? Might it even be a version of the sexual?'[12] But the high point of Kappeler's case is reached in the chapter 'Playing in the Literary Sanctuary' in which she describes the journal *La Nouvelle Critique*, the literary critical work based on the writings of Lacan, Barthes and Derrida.

> *La Nouvelle Critique* sees itself as constituting a radical break from [the literary] tradition. It hails the 'death of the author' and the birth of the reader. Its object is the pursuit, the exploration of pleasure, of desire. Not only the author–subject finds fulfilment in the medium, satisfaction of self-expression, but the reader too enjoys, *jouit*, engages in the process 'actively', wants it too, the pleasure, the orgasm, the *jouissance*.[13]

Kappeler goes on to connect the writer–author with the 'white man, author of the murder of Thomas Kasire' who

> puts himself inside the picture, dramatizes himself as hero in the represented scenario. Through his position within that picture, he offers the viewer a locus for identification, where the reader can join him as subject, to 'write' and compose the picture with him, to construct his pleasure and not to take notice of another possible locus for identification, that of the victim–object. For the reader, formally recipient in the literary scenario, servant to the author, now writes the text with him, helps produce the orgasm, produces the text, produces the *jouissance*, the meaning.'[14]

Nowhere does Kappeler state that: all representation is pornographic. But that is not her style. Her style is rhetoric, suggestion, analogy, persuasion. It suggests a complicity between representation in general and pornography. The underlying picture presented by her is this: men are the authors and readers of representational artefacts. Women are the objects represented. Men, the authors and the readers, derive pleasure from their objectification of women, and this pleasure is precisely the pleasure of pornography. In pornography, as in representation in general, men derive pleasure from the objectification of women. Men and pornographers are thus bracketed together.[15]

So there is a quite specific ambiguity in Kappeler's main thesis. Either representation in general should be the target, not pornography specifically, because pornography is only a special case of representation in general; or representation should be the target because all representation is pornographic. Although in both these cases, the range of objects covered by her attack is the same – the class of representations – the type of critique would be very different in each case. In the latter case, it is specifically the treating of women's bodies as the focus for male sexual pleasure that is the object of attack; in the former, representations are criticized only on the ground that they objectify women. Both these global claims are false. It is neither the case that all representations objectify women, nor that representations invariably present women as the objects of male desire. Kappeler would agree. She points to cases of women as the cultural authors and the readers. But these, she believes, are the exceptions in a culture in which men are the literary subjects and women are its objects. 'Culture is patriarchy's self-image',[16] Kappeler says, and she takes this to an extreme. She quotes a 'real-life situation' described by Deirdre English:

> One of the more erotic sights I ever saw was years ago at a feminist conference. It was a hot summer day in Pennsylvania, and during a break in the weekend-long conference, we gathered at an outdoor swimming pool. There were no men around, so we all stripped and swam naked – dozens of women, most of them perfect strangers ... The effect was incredibly beautiful.[17]

English is in the business of attempting to construct 'positive erotic images' for women, and this is one. Here is Kappeler on English:

> How does English imagine men 'see' feminist conferences, even when these are on a cold day and there is no swimming pool? How have men (pornographers) seen so many convents and girls schools? And how would a representation of such a scene, produced by a woman eroticist, fare in the world of representations?

This exchange is illustrative of Kappeler's tendency to abstract all representations from the context of their production and reception. The image described by English is written by a feminist and is intended (one presumes) for a largely feminist audience. Kappeler removes it from this context and transplants it to the world of male pornography. To do this is precisely what a feminist, in another context, criticizes a male pornographer for doing. Marianne Valverde describes a book about the emergent lesbian sexuality of a group of nuns, intended for a feminist/lesbian audience and written by lesbian ex-nuns. Valverde[18] tells us that this book was appropriated by the Canadian pornographic magazine *Forum*, and used as a jumping board for male sexual pleasure. The book was not written for *Forum* or for *Forum*'s readers. Feminists obviously should criticize the editors of *Forum* for taking up the piece in a misleading way. Their so doing might help increase awareness on the part of *Forum*'s readers of the impropriety of 'stealing' images from a feminist context. For Kappeler to imply, as she does, that all feminist writing, like that of English or the ex-nuns, is liable to be 'read' in the pornographic/patriarchal context of *Forum*, is to render impotent feminist critique of specific wrongs like the one Valverde describes.

Additionally, the corollary of Kappeler's view is that feminist attempts to present alternative erotica and to subvert the patriarchal genre are doomed to failure. For all of them are produced in a culture in which 'men are the subjects' and 'women are the objects.' It seems surprising, then, that Kappeler should say in the postscript to her book that 'the point is ... making possible a different practice, of seeing, of questioning, of critique, of infidelity to the dominant vision, of hollowing out from within.'[19] Is that not precisely what English, along with feminist novelists, is attempting to do?

There is a further point to be made. Kappeler urges that feminists move from looking at pornography as a special case of sexuality, to viewing it as representation. (Either as representation in general, or as a type of representation.) True, the pictures in *Penthouse* are representations of women. But they are representations of women in erotic poses, and intended to arouse a male audience sexually. This is not the case with representations of women in *Tom Jones*, *Jane Eyre* or Shakespeare's *Macbeth*. To shift the focus away from the sexual content of pornographic representations to representation in general is to miss the opportunity to criticize the eroticization of women's bodies in pornography.

Indeed, to elide different representational forms, as Kappeler does, is to subvert her attempts to escape the individualist perspective. To suggest, as she does, that 'men' are the authors and readers of representational artefacts, and women its objects, is to forget about the role of class and race. These complicate any perspective which has men in the position of power and women as the powerless victims.

Kappeler, therefore, does not fulfil her promise of escaping from the individualist tradition.

I would like to finish this chapter on Kappeler with a critique of her view that men are the cultural authors and women the objects. She suggests throughout her book that men, the subjects, turn another subject, women, into an object, thus robbing women of their subjectivity. 'In cultural historical terms it is the male gender, united by a common sense, who assumes the subject position, as the authors of culture, men assume the voice, compose the picture, write the story, for themselves and other men, and *about* women.' In the next chapter I will look at a literary genre that contradicts this view. It is a genre produced almost exclusively and for women. And it is not a one-off product like those of Jane Austen or Charlotte Brontë, it is the mass-cultural product of romantic fiction. But for the moment suppose we allow Kappeler her assumptions, that is, suppose that there is no women's representation *en masse*, and that any one-off product that may come on the scene, is liable to be appropriated by 'patriarchal culture'. I believe, even in these circumstances, that her perspective on the relation between subject and object cannot be right, for it is self-refuting.

In *The Phenomenology of Mind*,[20] Hegel describes the passage from organic life to properly human existence. He argues that self-consciousness emerges out of desire and its satisfaction. The subject needs some object – the child needs milk for example – and therefore experiences himself as lacking it. Thus self-consciousness begins to come about. The awareness of dependency on the object, however, 'negates' this emergent selfhood. Physical objects, Hegel argues, cannot be the means for maintaining the self-consciousness of a self because the satisfaction of the need leads to the removal of the 'lack' that the need represented. According to Hegel, only when desire or need is directed towards another desiring or needy subject can self-consciousness properly develop. Only a desiring subject, and not a physical object, can 'negate' itself without giving up its alterity. Self-consciousness is therefore dependent upon the mutual recognition of consciousnesses. In *Phenomenology* Hegel posits that one subject tries to subject the other's will to its own. His claim is that no self-consciousness will turn 'the other' into an object and nothing but an object, for, according to the above argument, that other is required for the subject's own self-consciousness. We can see this dynamic in the relationship between mother and child: the child needs the mother's recognition in order for it to begin to see itself as a self. Any subject needs another subject in order to be aware of him or herself as a self.

Kappeler, by contrast, believes that men, as the cultural authors and the cultural audience, create and consume representations of women as cultural objects. Men look at themselves through looking at women: 'The history of representation is the history of the male gender representing itself to itself.'[21] In other words, men gain self-consciousness and self-awareness by looking at women as objects. Men gain an awareness of self through their representation of women's view of them. But, and this is where Kappeler differs from Hegel, their representation of women is of women as objects. Is it possible that women could be solely objects? If men use women as the means through which they attain self-consciousness, these women must surely have some subject status. If women are nothing but objects, men cannot use them to acquire self-consciousness.

Kappeler and her sympathizers might respond that when she says that culture is patriarchy's self-image, she does not mean that men use women as their means of gaining self-consciousness, in general, but only that they use their representation of women as a means of reinforcing their 'patriarchal' power. But it is precisely through an individual man's experience of one woman in particular – his mother – that his sense of himself as a self and as a gendered self emerges. It is through his relationship to his mother that his awareness of his potential power begins to come into being. For Kappeler, however, 'the mother' is just one more patriarchal representation of woman. Again we see the contradiction: if the mother is to fulfil the role required of her by 'the patriarch', she must be more than an object. If she is nothing but an object, she cannot fulfil her role.

Finally, Kappeler is plagued by the same kind of difficulty to which as we saw in Chapter 1, Shulamith Firestone's writing is party. I suggested there that if one argues, as Firestone does, that 'sex/class' is the fundamental social divide affecting all social relations, and if one advocates, as she does, the elimination of this inequality, then one is *ipso facto* proposing the eradication of all social and political values – including values like liberty and autonomy – which the system supports. Kappeler's outlook suffers from a similar problem. For her, as we have seen, 'patriarchal' values penetrate ubiquitously. 'The mother' is a patriarchal invention, Deirdre English's attempt to create positive erotic images for women is suffused with the influence of patriarchy. It follows that liberal-democratic values are similarly affected and should also be eradicated. For why should this aspect of patriarchal society escape its all-invasive power?

Not only has Kappeler not fully left the individualist tradition behind, but her system of thought does not allow her to be sympathetic to the liberal values that we need to view in a more favourable light.

Conclusion

Rather than focusing on examples of women's art and women's representation as a way of countering Kappeler's thesis, I have pressed the limits of her arguments in her own terms. It is easy to say that Kappeler exaggerates because she underestimates the power that some men have over other men – white over black, middle class over working class, to give some obvious examples. This is a fair criticism, I believe, but I have chosen instead to look at the ambiguities and tensions in her argument. In the end, Kappeler's blanket view of the relation between men and women and representation in general downplays class and race differences and thus belies the promise of her book to attach equal importance to each of these notions. Like Dworkin and Griffin, therefore, Kappeler remains inside the presuppositions of the individualist tradition by refusing to attach sufficient weight to all relevant collectives.

9

Romantic Fiction: Porn for Women

All three feminist writers whose views I have examined share the view that pornography is a male preserve that exploits and uses women. This assumption is a mistaken one. As we see here, the romantic fiction of Mills and Boon is porn for women.

Millions of women read Mills and Boon novels and have done so for some years. According to one researcher, more Mills and Boon novels are read than books from any other publisher, and of the total Mills and Boon readership, the vast majority are women.[1] The same researcher's results show that while 28 per cent of all women read Mills and Boon, only 1 per cent of all men do so. About four and a half million women are regular subscribers. The company issues twelve new titles a month, each one containing about 200 pages of escapist stories. Every title has a print run of over 100,000, with many authors selling several million.

In the last few years in the USA and UK, there has been a mushroom growth in the number of critical works on romantic fiction.[2] Several writers have argued that romantic fiction is pornography for women.[3] I believe that the argument is still not widely accepted and I propose to present my own version of it in this chapter.

Why do so many women read romantic novels? Ann Douglas argues that their popularity represents a backlash against feminism.[4] But, as Janet Radway has pointed out, the growth in popularity of romance fiction in recent years has also been paralleled by changing marketing techniques and an improvement in the technology of production and distribution.[5] Part of the answer, then, I believe, is that almost any contemporary western woman, whatever her occupation, class background, ethnicity, or education, can identify with the heroines. And this does not just include the USA and Europe. The romances are read in Brazil, Israel, and, I found from my research, by West Indian and Asian women in Britain. They also thrive in Saudi Arabia and Japan.

Though the heroines are invariably white, and are sometimes identified as British or American, features like these are downplayed.

Qualities that make for differences among women are marginal; what is important is their femininity. Great significance is attached to the appearance and the clothes of the heroine. Often these are dazzling. 'She wore an orchid pink silky dress, strapped sandals with high heels in a matching kid, and [carried] two of Teresita's expensive cases ...'[6] Abigail, the heroine of another novel, sports hair the colour of 'ripe, glossy, chestnuts'.[7]

The emphasis on appearance is not to say, however, that the heroines are characterless. On the contrary, though this, once more, is played down, the heroines usually (even in the relatively early Mills and Boon novels) have a job; they are distinct personalities. Indeed, the company tells would-be writers that the characters 'should be convincing in both their actions and their words.'[8] Though the heroines are attractive, they are not princesses or goddesses; they are 'ordinary' women with 'ordinary' preoccupations. If they become rich – and many of the heroines do – it is by marrying wealth; and any of us can do *that,* can't we? Thus we can, in our mind's eye, overcome our inadequacies.

Appearance ultimately gives way to the inner fantasy of the heroine. It's not who she is, what she does or where she is that matters – it's her consciousness, and here the focus of her thoughts is her anticipation of romantic attachment. Now we are moving towards the reason why millions of women find Mills and Boon so compelling. The romance takes on a certain set pattern. Early on, the heroine despises her hero, often because of some typically masculine, macho, animal-like quality of his. In *Jacintha Point*, Laurel hates the macho Diego Ramirez; Dina, in *Strange Bedfellow*, dislikes the 'part primitive' Blake. Often, too, there is some other, less forcefully masculine, less dominant male in the background, whom she believes she loves. Sometimes, this man functions as a kind of friend to her (she has no real female friends).

The very features of the heroine's man which cause her to hate him initially draw her irresistibly towards him and cause her to fall uncontrollably, insatiably, in love. There is not even an obvious paradox here. The initial revulsion makes things respectable for the reader. 'Nice' women don't fall in love with powerful, unscrupulous, macho men. More importantly, each stage is part of the build-up to excitement: the initial dislike, the gradual transformation into sudden unlikely sparks of uncontrollable attraction, followed by the hero's attraction to the heroine, and culminating in the final stage of consummate passion. The anticipation and the waiting are necessary to the final successful outcome. Once the seal of the hero's love for the heroine and their marriage is fixed (the constraints some societies have required), she can abandon herself totally to her own unrelenting, inexorable passion.

Sexuality, of course, is universal – universally exciting. For romance to be exhilarating, the story must be set somewhere idyllic. The novels are sometimes located in specific places. *Jacintha Point*, by Elizabeth Graham, takes place in Mexico; *Isle of The Rainbows*, by Anne Hampson, in the Caribbean; *Wild Inheritance*, by Margaret Pargeter, is set on the west coast of Scotland. What matters is that the settings are far-away, dreamy, and beautiful. 'Camilla gazed out over the dreamy peace of the Bay of Islands as seen from the sheltered inlet of Rickorogi, the Gate of Heaven.'[9] In *Jacintha Point*, the Mexico we find ourselves in is not a divided society of a desperately poor peasantry and tiny wealthy elite, but an exotic land of 'tranquil vistas', 'jewel-toned skies' and 'hot sand'. *Isle of the Rainbows* is set in Dominica, again without the poverty. Our heroine awakes 'to a golden sunrise' and looks down at the garden 'blazing with colour, much of which comes from the trees ... the sweetly scented frangipani with its red and pink flowers, and the majestic shower of gold.'[10]

Though they are far from the centre stage, class background, ethnicity and age are present in typical ways. The heroine is invariably younger than the hero; she is also usually poorer. The hero is often 'foreign'; he frequently hails from societies that are more overtly patriarchal than the heroine's own culture. Indeed, there are sometimes elements of racism in the characterization of the hero. Mexico is more overtly patriarchal than England, parts of the Caribbean (from whence come many of the dark, macho heroes) more so than most parts of North America. These qualities add to the excitement; the older, richer, more macho and powerful the hero, the more he is like the 'black beast', and the more desirable he becomes to the heroine.

Readers have responded in a number of research projects to the question 'Why do you read Mills and Boon?' in various ways. In one such project, one woman said that the romances 'enabled her to forget the strains of modern living.' She is a mother with five children and works as a part-time cook. Another woman said they gave her 'a satisfactory sense of a pleasant and hopeful existence'. A third, a Pakistani woman who had been reading the novels in English, explained that 'they helped her English vocabulary.' Others found them 'arousing'; one woman claimed them to be 'less addictive than valium'.

Thus the novels enable some women to forget the strains of modern life. But how do they do this? Why do women look to Mills and Boon romances for this, rather than to TV soap operas or other forms of popular fiction? In a pioneering article on romantic fiction written in 1982, David Margolies[11] argues that the reader of romantic fiction is the passive recipient of an ideology that confirms her in her oppression. Tania Modelski, too, sees the reader of romantic fiction as being in bad faith.[12] But this assumption of passivity on the part of the readers of romantic fiction is challenged in Janice Radway's study *Reading the Romance*. She argues that the text is not a fixed object, but has different layers of meaning. Readers therefore are not the passive recipients of data; rather they actively attribute significance to the words on the page on the basis of previously learned cultural codes. Instead of focusing on the texts, Radway analyses a group of readers' responses to them. Many of the answers to her questions confirm my view that behind the surface responses there is something else. Women find these novels gripping (and this was confirmed by my own research) because they are erotic. They are erotic in special ways. They play upon many women's unconscious fantasies; they feed, as Ann Snitow puts it, certain 'regressive elements in the female experience'.[13]

Some Mills and Boon authors now consciously style their novels as erotic, but even the others are full of sexual overtones. The heroine is usually sexually aroused throughout the story. Plot and characterization are ancillary to the question that has us on tenterhooks – will she or will she not get her man – and to the expectation of eventual sexual fulfilment.

If the pattern of the novels has changed over the last ten years (and it has, to an extent), it is in this respect: the sexuality has become more overt. Who can doubt the eroticism in passages like these from *Strange Bedfellow*?

Fire ignited at the hard pressure of his mouth, hungry and demanding. It spread through her veins, her bones melting under the intense heat ... His roaming hands caressed and shaped her ever closer to his solidly muscled flesh. Their combined body heat melted them together, fixing them with the glorious fire of their love. His driving male need made Dina aware of the empty aching in the pit of her stomach that only he could satisfy. Soon, the torrid embrace was not enough. It was unable to meet the insatiable needs of their desire... The initial storm of their passion was quickly spent. When Blake came to her a second time, their lovemaking was slow and langorous.[14]

There are differences, of course, from the more obviously erotic *Lady Chatterley's Lover*, but this is not because sexuality is absent in the Mills and Boon novel. It is more that sex and love are intertwined in it. Here is Lawrence:

> It was a night of sensual passion, in which she was a little startled and almost unwilling: yet pierced again with piercing thrills of sensuality, different, sharper, more terrible than the thrills of tenderness.[15]

The differences between *Lady Chatterley's Lover* and *Counterfeit Bride*, another Mills and Boon novel, certainly do not lie in the absence of eroticism in the latter. They lie in the lack of love and romance. In Lawrence's novel there are the swear words, rendered so infamous at the trial in 1961; Lawrence invokes Bacchic rituals, a 'human nature' that reaches below and beyond the ordinary lives of average human beings. Lawrence's sex is much closer to the essence of the action – a glorified sensuality, but none the less pure eroticism. In a Mills and Boon romance, sex is never present without fantasy, love and the possibility of marriage. But, as far as the description of sexuality itself goes, the similarities are more striking than the differences. For instance, the devices Lawrence uses to indicate excitement on Connie's part are analogous to those we find in Mills and Boon novels. Lawrence writes: 'She perceives a new nakedness emerging. And she was half afraid. Half she wishes he would not caress her so. He was encompassing her somehow. Yet she was waiting, waiting.'[16]

As I have already mentioned, waiting is all-important in Mills and Boon. The heroine initially rejects her man while also being powerfully drawn to him. Throughout the novels we are given hints of her excitement – her attraction to him when she encounters him, and his constant presence, whatever she is doing, in her thoughts. Each romance builds up to the culmination of marriage, love and sexual fulfilment; none of these elements can exist without the others. Passages from Mills and Boon that are not explicitly sexual are often implicitly so. Ann Snitow suggests that we should read the expression 'hard fingers' in one Harlequin romance as the penis. Indeed, romance is itself often a metaphor for sexual excitement. Men are reputed to gain excitement of a sexual sort from warfare, from car chases; the source of excitement on offer for women is romance. As Snitow puts it: 'when women try to picture excitement, society offers them one vision, romance ... when women try to fantasize about success, mastery, the society offers them one vision: the power to attract a man.'[17]

The sort of explicit sex in *Strange Bedfellow*, written in 1979, is absent from the *Isle of the Rainbows*, written a decade earlier. Even the titles indicate the difference of emphasis. Yet the theme is the same: our heroine initially hates her hero, loathing the very qualities that cause her to fall for him in the end. And there is eroticism very early on in the novel. Even though the heroine, Penny, can at first find nothing about her hero to like, contact between them is sexualized: 'The second dressing was applied; Max's hands were on her shoulders as he pressed the dressing firmly into place. At the unexpected action an odd quiver swept through her and, to her utter dismay, Max became aware of it.'[18] We are given a vivid description of Max's masculinity: 'His straight black brows added to the impression of hardness, as did his hair, which was thick and strong.'[19]

Unlike the sexuality of the stories in *Penthouse* or *Playboy*, the eroticism in Mills and Boon is never explicitly about penetration: there is no stark description of the sexual act. Full sex, if it takes place at all, is always implicit. It is the embrace, not the sexual act itself, that expresses the male's torrid sensuality. Not only this, but it is often not actual sexual behaviour that is erotic. The novels are exciting not because they give detailed accounts of scenes in the bedroom, but because of the ways in which they play upon sexual desires and sexual fantasies. Passages like those quoted above, paragraphs containing electric metaphors and descriptions of 'torrid sensuality', are in the minority in the Mills and Boon romance. Instead, we have passages like this: 'he emitted vibrations from up there on the black horse, vibrations of mastery and mystery. Jane felt her heart was beating too fast.'[20] The heroines of Mills and Boon novels are overwhelmed by sexual desire, and it is a particular sort of sexual desire. The woman is not the initiator. In her fantasy, she always responds. She is excited, in her fantasies, by the hero's response to her body. She desires to be desired. She is passive, freed from responsibility for her own feelings, absolved from accountability for her own sexuality. In all these respects the Mills and Boon heroine is playing the part of the ideal woman in many cultures today.

Sometimes the lovemaking is a scene of rape. The hero is brutally dominant. But it is rape in which the woman submits and enjoys sex. In *Bought with His Name*, the heroine feels 'exquisite pain'; in *Strange Bedfellow*, she 'loses control' and 'willingly lets his lips dominate hers for as long as he chooses.' He is choosing, but she gratefully, joyously accepts his choice. She is passive and accepting;

he is powerful, dominant and initiating. Even where his power is mitigated by love and a desire for marriage, it is still strongly present. The heroes are macho, dominant and overridingly in control of their emotions and their situations. In *Jacintha Point*, Laurel is rendered unconscious by a blow on the head, and loses her memory after her first passionate encounter with the ardent Mexican, Diego. He subsequently controls her. In *Unguarded Moment* by Sara Craven, Liam is the artful yet supremely rational male who is able to expose and destroy women. Alix, the heroine, is a 'little fool'.[21] The male is experienced, the one who knows how to dominate; the female is inexperienced, new to it all. She can only respond with desire to please the hero.

The 'hard pressure' of Blake's mouth in *Strange Bedfellow*, the 'torrid assault' of his desire and 'his driving male need', are paler versions of a type of pornographic writing epitomized by *Apartment House Sex Killer* by Jack Thomas: 'He slipped his huge dagger-like dick into her mouth. He rammed it relentlessly inside her, driving it with forceful energy.'[22] The story involves the murder of a woman by slashing her breasts with a knife. *Strange Bedfellow*, by contrast, ends happily in marriage. But despite the different degrees of sadomasochism involved, both stories are about dominance, relative power on the part of the male, and submission by the female. Both involve violation of the 'personhood' of both sexes in the sense described in the last chapter.

The irony in another Mills and Boon romance, *Isle of the Rainbows*, clearly exaggerates the truth; none the less there *is* truth behind the joke:

> And then one lovely evening, when Max was sitting by her bedside, holding her hand and looking at her with a tenderness she would never have believed possible, he asked her to marry him. 'That is', he added with some amusement, 'if you can bring yourself to live with a pompous, conceited ass, a super-being who is insufferably arrogant and full of his own importance ...'
>
> 'Max ... don't!'
>
> '... a man who is totally without feeling or compassion, whose god is money ...'[23]

Though Max is self-critical and self-parodying, he is like the representation of himself, and it is these very qualities that his girlfriend Penny loves in him. Independence is permissible to an increasing degree in the recent romances; the woman is even permitted to think that marriage is not what she is really after: 'There are more things in life than romance and marriage.'[24] But we soon find out that this thought is a self-delusion; Camilla, another Mills and Boon heroine, really wants only marriage in the end. Mention is even made of movements that challenge these social norms: 'The woman's movement isn't the whole answer, you know.'[25] Sexuality in these novels confirms and extends the role of the 'feminine' woman and the 'masculine' man. The men are powerful, aggressive and independent. Barbara Cartland employs the same imagery:

> He crushed her to him and his lips found hers. He kissed her brutally with a violence which seemed to force the very life from between her lips. She wanted to gasp for air, but his arms held her closer and closer. She felt her lips quiver beneath his, she felt as if his mouth conquered her, possessed her utterly so that she had no longer any identity of her own but was a part of him ... She could only feel that burning, passionate, possessive kiss upon her lips – a kiss which seemed to have seared its way right into her very soul.[26]

The traditional feminine role of the woman is made to appear compelling and exciting through being made sensual. All of this is essential to pornographic sexuality. The woman does her utmost to make herself desired, doing all those things that are part and parcel of her submissive role but enjoying them because they might attract a man. Her sexuality is expressed as submission – she does not so much desire as desire to be desired. Despite their being 'bathed in romance', Mills and Boon novels are pornographic. They are pornographic precisely because like *Penthouse* or *Playboy* they eroticize domination. Pornography is, I believe, representational material which eroticizes domination and which is used to stimulate sexual arousal. Marianne Valverde concurs with my view.[27] She argues that porn not only eroticizes domination of one sex by another; class domination is eroticized as well. But romantic fiction is also pornographic according to Rosalind Coward's definition: '[it] puts into circulation images of sexuality that have definite meanings associated with them: sexual pleasure for men is initiation and dominance and for women it is submission to men's depersonalised needs.'[28] As I suggested earlier, the perceived role of the female model in hard-core porn is just like that of the Mills and Boon heroine. The model is perceived as wanting a man to desire her; one model desired a romantic figure, a man who 'has something in his head [who is] sympathetic.'[29]

In *The Female Eunuch*, Germaine Greer exhorts women to give up the 'moony fantasies' of romance for the 'virile, no-nonsense brand of sexuality' of real pornography.[30] Women should treat romance with irony and cynicism, she says; real porn gets rid of romance. But as we have seen here, women have combined porn and romance.

A word of caution may be appropriate. I earlier criticized Dworkin and others for exaggerating the meaning of the term 'violent'; I also objected to Kappeler's extension of the pornographic to representation in general. Am I not here dangerously extending the notion of the pornographic? Is there not a likelihood that the concept might have too wide an application? I believe that this is not so, for, unlike Dworkin and Kappeler, I have provisionally defined what counts as pornography and have restricted its application.

Can There be a Pornography for Women?

Until very recently, those who asked this question replied in the negative. In *Women, Sex and Pornography*, Beatrix Faust informed us that 'most women have no interest in pornography.'[31] For, she said, 'if [a woman] is eager to read her man's *Playboy*, *Penthouse* or *Hustler*, she may get sidelong glances from people ...'

Recently, however, feminists have recognized that women sometimes find pornography erotic, even pornography depicting violence against women. Maria Marcus,[32] in *A Taste for Pain*, describes many women who masochistically enjoy being the object of violence. And Marion Bower[33] cites a study which suggests that, despite the fact that women are socially conditioned against responding to sexually explicit material, many women do respond erotically to pornographic material. This suggests, she argues, that there is something within women which either resists or overrides social conditioning.

No doubt there are women who respond erotically to images of violence. Yet there are far more female readers of Mills and Boon romantic fiction than there are female viewers of violent sex videos, for instance. And surely, for the majority of women at least, it is likely that domination by a man will appear in the guise of love; powerful masculinity will be seen as romance. Scenes which in another context would be described unreservedly as rape will be bathed in the romance of the marriage vows. But with these vows, a woman can tell herself that domination is all about courtship and romance; she can pretend to herself each time she reads a novel that she is re-enacting her own courtship, or experiencing something she missed.

Mills and Boon novels are not propaganda; they do not shape attitudes. Unlike women's magazines in the Second World War, which were vehicles for propaganda, Mills and Boon novels are too bland for that. To say, moreover, as one commentator did,[34] that they are 'ideological' and that they present a particular model of behaviour as 'natural', seems too strong. Certainly, they do not offer the reader any alternative to love and marriage, and they probably would not succeed as romances if they did. But their views not only of love and relationships, but of 'normal' masculinity and femininity, are fantasies and, as such, they differ from a simple reproduction of real life and the presentation of any aspect of it as 'natural'. Rather than making a certain pattern of behaviour seem natural, they allow women to imagine that love and romance along the lines of the novels are possible: that these things can really happen to the unhappy housewife.

Mills and Boon novels present women in ways which often deny to them independence, autonomy and rationality; none the less, women who read them are not to be condemned as the witless dupes of an evil ideology. That would be left-wing moralizing of the worst kind. Mills and Boon allow women to imagine that they can perform properly the part of the feminine woman. Mills and Boon present the world, as *Jane Eyre* does, through the eyes of the woman.

In them, the role of the feminine woman appears bathed in glory; it comes across in the most favourable light possible. Like *Penthouse* and *Playboy*, Mills and Boon play upon fantasy. In the end, what Mills and Boon novels suggest is the possibility of being successfully feminine. In reality, no woman can really be a successful 'romantic' virgin and a perfect nurturer. 'Femininity', it turns out, is a cultural stereotype which no woman can live up to.

If romantic fiction is a form of pornography in which women appear to be the subjects, a pornography that is produced and consumed by women, then the view of Dworkin, Griffin and Kappeler – that pornography is exclusively a male preserve – is undermined. Even though the heroines of the romances are, in some respects, like the women in the pages of *Penthouse*, it is not men who are treating them as their fantasy objects. The Mills and Boon heroine, although object to her hero, is also the subject of the novel and subject for the reader. Most Mills and Boon novels are written by women. Women, therefore, in this case, are the 'cultural authors' and the 'cultural audience'.

We cannot, however, let matters rest here. Why do women concur in their object status? Why do so many women read Mills and Boon romantic fiction?

The Popularity of Romance: A Freudian Explanation

Several critics have offered Freudian explanations for the popularity of romantic fiction.[35] They argue along the following lines.

The reader of Mills and Boon romances identifies with the heroine. Drawing on Freud's writings, it is argued that the reader/heroine, in fantasy, becomes like a child, a child who desires and is loved by the powerful, absent father. In her fantasy she sees herself as he will see her. She identifies both with the heroine and with the hero's perception of her as beautiful and desirable. Here we have the actions of a father towards his child, or perhaps the longed-for actions of the father towards her in the child's fantasy. The hero is invariably older than the heroine – like the reader's father. He is quite often richer than she – richer in this sense suggesting someone more sophisticated, more experienced, more worldly – again like the reader's father.

Underlying this Freudian reading is another interpretation. Who has actually adored the Mills and Boon reader in the way she wants her hero to love her heroine? It is not her father; for most of us, it is our mothers or female caretakers who love us in this way. Thus the reader of the Mills and Boon romance also becomes the child desiring her mother. It is the mother or the female carer who, in reality, controls the identity of the child. It is the mother to whom the child belongs in the early years. Thus, although the macho, powerful heroes of the Mills and Boon romances are male, for the child they also represent the mother.

One could go further. According to Freud, children of both sexes have both active and passive sexual aims. The little girl actively desires her mother: 'active wishful impulses directed towards the mother regularly arise in girls during the phallic phase.' Sometimes, Freud argues, the social obstacles to women's realizing these aims lead to their turning them against themselves; they introject them so that they are expressed as depression or misery. Depression is triggered, in Freud's view, by the unconscious experience of disappointment at the inability to realize one's aims. But instead of directing their anger at the person or persons supposedly responsible for their loss, depressed individuals direct it against these persons internalized within the self. A version of this surely explains women's fantasies of being raped. They turn against themselves their own fantasies of anger towards men. Reading Mills and Boon romantic fiction, then, could be seen as a strong and independent affirmation of activity in contrast to the passivity and self-destruction of depression. The woman reading Mills and Boon becomes like the child who, in addition to having passive sexual aims, has active ones; she actively desires to seek her man's desire.

Thus by reading Mills and Boon novels women may be simultaneously concurring in their own subordination and being strong and independent. Woman are neither, as Dworkin and Kappeler tend to assume they are, simply objects nor simply emancipated intellectuals. As I argued earlier, most women combine something of both qualities. Reading romantic fiction may be a reflection of the ambiguous and difficult situation in which many women find themselves today.

In a way, as Alison Light[36] argues about Daphne du Maurier's *Rebecca*, the romantic fiction novel exposes the myth of the full and coherent self (Dworkin's emancipated female self or Kappeler's male subject). The texts themselves, as well as the readers' responses to them, expose the doubts and delusions surrounding a woman's desire in heterosexual sexual relationships, as well as the ambiguities and ambivalences of the feminine role in general. We might go so far as to say that the idea of a whole, fully rounded self is not only one to which most women today do not have access, but that it is not in any event a desirable end. Those feminists like Mary Daly who, as I argued earlier, paint a glowing picture of a state in which women are whole pure feminists are surely describing a state that is both unreal and undesirable. In so far as they express the conflicts and ambiguities in a woman's sense of self, Mills and Boon novels represent worthy alternatives to unrealizable and undesirable feminist 'dystopias'.

Earlier I mentioned that some feminists have begun to discuss women's erotic response to violent pornography. We can fit this positive response to violent porn into our picture of romantic novels. Marion Bower[37] analyses the erotic response of both women and men to violent porn in which both sexes play both sadistic and masochistic roles by means of a Kleinean analysis of the sadistic fantasies of babies. As Bower points out, Freud himself saw an intimate connection between cruelty and the sex instinct. He suggested that masochism was a secondary derivative of primary sadism which had been denied outward expression and had been turned inward, taking the self as its object. Melanie Klein, a psychoanalyst working after Freud, believed that both destructive and masochistic instincts were present in the child from very early on. Before the child has properly differentiated itself from its mother, she (the mother) is experienced (internalized) both as a 'good object' that satisfies the child's needs, and as a 'bad object' that frustrates its desires. Thus, the child may behave sadistically towards its mother – it will sometimes bite its mother's breasts or fantasize scooping out their entire contents. Klein also discusses the use of urine and faeces – the child's only 'gifts' – as instruments of torture. Bower mentions instances of pornography that re-enact these fantasies.

Bower therefore claims that violent pornography is arousing for women for many of the same reasons as it is for men. She then goes on to ask why it is that more women are not aroused by sadistic porn. Her answer is that whereas heterosexual men (on the Kleinean analysis) retain their first object – a woman – heterosexual women change their object. Since women are the object of the earliest and most intensely sadistic fantasies, it is not surprising, Bower claims, that those who retain women as their object should have a particular interest in the types of images portrayed by much violent porn. But there is, in addition, the obvious point that Bower does not mention, which is that if identification with another of the same sex is as strong as Freudian and Kleinean theory makes it out to be, then it is obviously harder for the woman to identify with a male sadist acting out his fantasies on a woman victim than it is for the man.

Bower analyses the purpose of violent pornography by arguing that certain painful early experiences may become sexualized and re-enacted as sexual fantasies. The effect of this is that the original 'psychic pain and rage' is lost. But there arises a compulsive need to repeat the fantasy in an attempt to regain and master the earlier experience. Sadistic and masochistic pornographic fantasies, says Bower, can be traced back to this need. One could extend Klein's work and suggest that these early experiences may sometimes have been fantasies.

Bower may have a point in her analysis of women's responses to violent porn, but it remains true that romantic fiction is far more popular and widely read than any violent pornographic magazine. And, although these psychoanalytic explanations go some way towards explaining the popularity of women's pornography, they do not on their own account for the phenomenon. Like the porn industry, romance too is big business. Part of the motivation for authors to write the novels in question (some authors write one a month) is profitability. Thus once more a class dimension enters the picture.

Indeed, as with my critique of Griffin in Chapter 7, these psychoanalytic readings of women's responses to Mills and Boon and to violent porn, must be taken with a pinch of salt. Not all women are brought up by their mothers, and some may not have experienced the 'absent' father. Too great a reliance on psycho-analytic theory for the explanation of the popularity of romantic fiction could lead us back to the individualist perspective by, once more, abstracting the child–parent relationship from its social context.

Conclusion

In this chapter I have argued against the assumption held by Kappeler, Dworkin and Griffin that porn is a male preserve. On the contrary, Mills and Boon romantic fiction is widely disseminated, and it is porn for women. I will have more to say in the next chapter about the consequences of this.

10
Porn and Autonomy

'Your hands are not your own, nor are your breasts, nor, most especially, any of your bodily articles, which we may explore or penetrate at will ... you have lost all right to privacy or concealment, and ... will never close your lips completely, or press your knees together.'[1] The central female character of *The Story of O* is raped, systematically tortured and objectified by her oppressors. The clothes she wears define her function – as object, as orifice – for her possessors. Her clothes expose her breasts and genitalia. They also serve as an apparatus of constraint and discipline, training O to stand up straight, to project breasts, buttocks, stomach. Whip-lashes criss-cross her body.

In Anne-Marie's house (one of the residences in the story) O and other women are suspended on a dais, their buttocks and spread legs in the air, their genitalia exposed to the torturer's whip. They are visible only as buttocks and spread thighs. Their faces cannot be seen. They are open simultaneously to penetration and torture.

The women in *The Story of O* are utterly complicit in their suffering: O thanks her torturers after each whipping. Her loss of subjectivity is so great that 'lying motionless on her back, her loins still aflame ... [O] had the feeling that by some strange substitution Sir Stephen was speaking for her, in her place.'[2] *The Story of O* is written as though O demands her chastisement.

In earlier chapters I criticized the liberal and radical feminist outlooks on porn. I agree with radical feminists that porn is to be condemned and that it is open to condemnation centrally because of its portrayal of women. The view of what is wrong with porn, developed in this chapter, expands on an idea that is very much in the forefront of radical feminist writing. Additionally, I employ a concept – autonomy – that is central in liberal thinking.

De Sade's heroines and heroes are even more extreme than O. As Battaille puts it, de Sade 'makes his heroes uniquely self-centred, the partners are denied any rights at all: this is the key for his system.'[3] De Sade's heroes seek pleasure to excess. Yet, in so doing, any real emotion is lost. To quote again from Battaille: 'Jules Janin wrote of de Sade's books [that]

> there are bloody corpses everywhere, infants torn from their mothers' arms, young women with their throats slit after an orgy, cups full of blood and wine, unimaginable tortures ... In his first book (*La Nouvelle Justine*), he shows us a poor girl at bay, lost, ruined, shrinking under a rain of blows, led by inhuman monsters through one underground vault after another ... When the author has committed every crime there is, when he is sated with incest and monstrosities ... then at last this man pauses, looks at himself, smiles to himself and is not frightened.[4]

Appropriate emotions disappear. Juliette is cool and reflective in her pursuit of domination. The libertine who lives for pleasure loses his capacity for pleasure.

De Sade's heroes pursue objectification to the limit. They destroy the objects of their passions. Yet, as Bataille points out, and as I argued in Chapter 8, denying others is ultimately to deny oneself. The libertine who cuts the throats of young women is cutting his own throat. In order to see why this is, let us look again at the passage from Hegel's *Phenomenology of Mind*, the master–slave dialectic.

The Master–Slave Relation

In this section of the *Phenomenology*, as we have seen,[5] Hegel is asking the question, 'How do I become aware of myself as a self?' He believes that 'desires' are important to the consciousness of our own existence. As people act on things because they want them – the child wants a teddy bear or something to eat – they begin to gain a sense of themselves as distinct from those objects. Hegel, however, argues that we cannot be fully aware of ourselves as selves unless we are conscious of other people. Here he is on the importance of the view of 'the other' to one's own sense of self: 'Self-consciousness exists in and for itself, in that, and by the fact that it exists for another self-consciousness; that *is* to say, it is only by being recognised.'[6]

Hegel suggests that we all aim to be recognized by others; wanting to be noticed by others, to be deemed worthy by others are traits we all have. Sometimes we identify with another and instead of seeing ourselves as independent autonomous subjects, we identify with Princess Diana, our headmistress or somebody successful at work. But, says Hegel, if my identity lies outside myself – in my head of department or my father – it is outside my control. Therefore, Hegel suggests, I, the jealous one, may set out to destroy the person in whom my 'selfhood' resides. Of course, few of us really set out to destroy someone of whom we are jealous; Hegel is describing the extreme limits of such a feeling. The conflict between myself and the person in whom my identity resides will become a struggle between life and death, Hegel suggests, because it is only by risking one's life that one becomes fully aware of oneself as a free, autonomous individual. It is only when I realize how fragile my life is, and what its limits are, that I can become a truly free person. However, we must remember an earlier passage from Hegel: the other person's attitude towards me is important for my sense of self-identity, he says. So I must neither die myself, nor must I destroy the individual in whom my identity resides.

Since we cannot go on struggling with one another indefinitely, Hegel says, one must submit to the other. The one who submits he calls the 'slave' and the one to whom that person submits him/her self becomes the 'master'. Thus we get dependence and independence of self-consciousness: master and slave. Hegel believes that the 'master–slave dialectic' is a phase in the development of world history, in the progression towards freedom of the 'Spirit' that controls historical change. In fact, the relationship is disadvantageous both for the slave and the master. Whereas the master fails to gain a proper sense of himself from the slave, the slave, because he or she merely carries out the master's will, does gain a certain degree of self-consciousness by means of the work he or she performs for the master. In pornography we can see the appropriateness of the master–slave dialectic. It captures the relation between O and her captors, Sir Stephen and Rene. O becomes like Hegel's slave: her identity lies in Sir Stephen. In much pornography, women (and sometimes men) become objects for another. They may literally become objects, as in men's pornographic publications dealing entirely with women's buttocks and anuses, breasts, legs or genitals. As in the case of O or Justine, they may become the object of male desire. O is largely the instrument of the satisfaction of Sir Stephen's wants. She is divested of personhood.

The philosopher J.P. Sartre believed that in the act of lovemaking the lover becomes at once subject and object: she sees herself partly as the body desired by her lover. But then her identity is partly outside her control, so she tries to turn her lover into an object as well. In pornography, one person becomes a body desired by the other, but this is not usually reciprocated. The woman is simply the object. She either involuntarily submits to this role (as does the woman on the pages of *Penthouse*) or she does it voluntarily, like O or Justine. Since the identity of the lover – the woman – becomes submerged in the other lover's desire for her/his body, one of the two may become afraid and want to kill the other. In a recent hard-core pornographic film from Denmark, the woman ends up killing the man. Throughout the film, the man forces the woman to act out his wishes and fantasies. His death at her hands seems metaphorical, but it fits the present idea: the person whose identity becomes submerged may want to kill the dominant other. Sometimes it is the man who kills the woman. In Norman Mailer's *American Dream*, for instance, the hero's wife, the slave, dies. De Sade said that if one wants to know about death one should look at sexual excitement. We have already mentioned that Freud, in *Beyond the Pleasure Principle*, described the 'drive to inorganicism' as the 'most' radical form of the pleasure principle'. Sexuality affords us the opportunity of transgressing the barrier separating life from death.

There are pornographic films in which these things do not happen, and in which women are depicted as gaining equal pleasure as men. However, for the responses of male and female viewers to be equivalent, we would have to live in a world in which men and women responded equally to visual sexual stimuli, and this is not the case. The greater importance of vision in male sexuality has been noted frequently,[7] and sometimes interpreted as a natural phenomenon. One writer has offered an evolutionary explanation: the man's desire to look at female genitals is part of the motivational process that maximizes male reproductive opportunities.[8] Alternatively, one might explain the phenomenon socially.

Even in porn, the taboo against killing is usually upheld. Instead we have the master–slave relation: one party is seen as the body desired by the other, but this desire is not reciprocated. Unlike Hegel's slave, however, who loses his or her subjectivity to the master, the 'slave' in porn must retain some subjectivity or she will cease being desirable to the master. Women are not only the objects of male desire; they play a part in their creation as such. There is a subjective aspect to 'being-as-object'. The subjectivity of the slave is as a subject who desires to be object – a subject who wants only to satisfy the wants of the master. She does not really become an object; rather, she is treated as a means of satisfying the man's desire.

Things ought not to be this way in lovemaking, however. People ought to treat one another as people, as autonomous beings, in lovemaking as elsewhere. One of the things wrong with porn, therefore, is that someone's – usually the woman's – autonomy is violated. The woman in porn becomes a means of satisfying the man's desires: she is not treated as an end. Even though O voluntarily submits, she is not autonomous. For, as we saw in Chapter 4, treating someone as an end involves acting on the basis of one's own wants and needs, wants and needs that have been rationally arrived at, when all constraints at achieving them have been removed. Among the constraints are such things as lack of information about the consequences of satisfying one's wants, but we also included such constraints as culture and lack of means. No rational person, acting on the basis of as full as possible information and in the absence of other constraints, would choose to be constantly subjected to torture. O is a figment of the imagination of her creator. It is wrong, therefore, to treat any individual in the way that O or Justine are treated.

A contrasting view is found in an important article by Jessica Benjamin.[9] Drawing on some of the literature already mentioned (Hegel, Freud, Bataille and others) Benjamin offers a reading of *The Story of O*. She argues that, for Battaille, the significance of eroticism is that it allows

> transgression of the most fundamental taboo, that separating life from death. Life means discontinuity, the confinement of each individual to a separate, isolated existence. Death means continuity; not life, each individual is united with the rest, sunk back into the sea of non-differentiation ... The body stands for discontinuity, individuality, life. Consequently, the violation of the body in erotic violation breaks the taboo between life and death and breaks through our discontinuity from the other. While this break is the hidden secret of all eroticism, it is most clearly expressed in erotic violation.[10]

Benjamin goes on to argue that, in *The Story of O*, O's masters find enjoyment not so much in their pleasure as in the fact that they can take it at all. They must maintain their separateness from O or they risk becoming dependent on her. Additionally, she argues, O's willingness to go all the way towards objectification expresses her efforts to win recognition from her idealized lovers, and thus to seek a kind of transcendence, an affirmation of her self (something that, as we have seen, Hegel argues is essential for the attaining of selfhood). Why, asks Benjamin, does O seek transcendence in this way, and not through the reciprocal giving of self? Her answer: 'were both partners to give up self and control, the disorganization of self would be total.'[11] 'It may be then, Benjamin says, 'that the primary motivation for maintaining inequality in the erotic relationship, and ultimately for establishing the master–slave constellation, is the fear of ego loss – the boundless.'[12]

In the end, Benjamin suggests that individualism, the insistence on boundaries, a focus on difference and polarity, as opposed to an emphasis on mutuality and interdependence is part of the 'western rational world view'.[13] This in turn can be partly explained, she suggests, as a result of women's responsibility for mothering. Presumably, she would argue, the loss of boundaries of selfhood would be feared less, in a society which placed less emphasis than 'the western rational world' on individuality and difference.

I believe, however, that if one adopts the conception of autonomy I have described, with its emphasis on 'other-directed' concerns and qualities, as well as a focus on the self, one's view about eroticism would be different. Eroticism, after all, is very different from death: unlike the latter it does not involve the annihilation of all boundaries. The experience of merging with the other always co-exists with a recognition of the separateness of oneself. I disagree, therefore, with Benjamin's assertion that the maintainance of transcendence in eroticism need be connected (even in western rational societies) with domination and submission. It is possible, despite the inequalities of sex, race and class to internalize aspects of the other in eroticism – to experience her or his concerns as one's own – without involving the annihilation of the self. Eroticism should involve each lover reciprocally recognizing the autonomy of the other: each party taking the other's wants as his or her own. Dominance and submission of necessity violate this relationship of mutual recognition and autonomy.

Pornography and Fantasy

Porn, however, involves fantasy. Goldstein and Kant say that porn merely causes people to have sexual ideas.[14] Susan Barrowclough argues that pornographic fantasizing is autonomous.[15] Indeed one argument against pornography is that it 'does our imagining for us'.[16] (Kenneth Tynan says that this is exactly what all writers do,[17] although another writer disagrees. Writers of good literature, he says, do not 'do our imagining for us'.)[18] Whatever the case may be, there appears, at least intuitively, to be nothing wrong with fantasizing treating the other purely as a means to the satisfaction of one's desires.

Chris Cherry[19] argues that there is: fantasy in itself can be wrong. He suggests that a certain type of fantasizing, what he calls 'idle' fantasizing, may be morally wrong. He distinguishes idle fantasy from 'surrogate' fantasy: 'fantasy is surrogate when it substitutes for an external – pre-existing and presupposed – desideratum. It is a *faute de mieux* for the real thing. By contrast it is idle when it is desired only within, and so remains an internal property of the fantasy.' He offers an example of surrogate fantasy:

> Ruth twice made love to an apparition of her husband Paul, who she deliberately created for that specific purpose ... Asked how satisfying the experience was sexually, she replied that it was very satisfying, and that the apparition would be a good substitute for Paul whenever he was away.

And of idle fantasy:

> The fantasies which I have always needed ... are for me far more tedious and obnoxious. In them I am always passive, objectified, humiliated and whatever abuse I can imagine to be happening at the time also contains the threat of even worse to follow ... I resent the content of the fantasies. And I resent the effort I have to make to produce them, and the disconnection which occurs with lovers who, at least recently, are most caring, gentle, and as extensively physically stimulating as I would wish ... The problem with masochistic fantasy, I find, is *not at all* that it encourages real submissiveness and most certainly not any desire for real pain, hurt or humiliation ...

Cherry, quoting Lynne Segal,[20] suggests that there are two obvious ways in which idle fantasy may be wrong, but he rejects both of these. They are: idle fantasy is wrong because of its consequences – idle fantasy about dominating another, for instance, makes one more likely to dominate others. Cherry can find no evidence for this. Alternatively, fantasy might be said to be wrong in so far as it postulates a world in which domination is acceptable, and this is in itself bad. Cherry objects: the idea of condemning something that occurs in a fantasy world is obscure. His suggestion is that idle fantasies are bad because they involve one in distancing oneself from the truth: 'The evil consists in the mismatch, the fissure between those wants a person has and gratifies only in fantasy and those he has, and may or may not gratify in reality.'[21] They also invariably concern the self: 'the activity is one in which the self always has itself in prospect, is at once self-absorbed and self-congratulatory. Those features cannot possibly exist with any sort of goodness.'

I disagree with Cherry, and my disagreement turns on the view of the self which I believe underlies his work. Cherry is critical of the 'mismatch' between 'idle' fantasy and real wants and desires, partly because of the self-indulgence of allowing free rein to fantasy wants, but also, I think, because he dislikes the idea of a 'dislocated', 'fragmented' self. The conception of the self to which he would be sympathetic would be one which is whole and unitary: a self whose desires are in harmony, and not one that holds contradictory beliefs. This conception of the self, as we have seen, underlies much philosophical and feminist writing: Descartes believed that the 'true' self would be revealed once the distorting veil of perception was removed; Mary Daly has advocated a 'true' women's self that emerges once patriarchal conditioning is lifted; Andrea Dworkin also holds this notion of the unitary self.

The trouble with the 'unitary self' is that it denigrates women's (and sometimes men's) actual experience. Women and men, but especially women, are subject to conflicting pressures, and are often expected to take on a number of different roles simultaneously. When Lynne Segal imagines herself in a masochistic role (à la Cherry's example), she condemns herself for having these fantasy wants. But surely she is only playing out the type of conflict experienced by many women in a society that expects them to play the nurturing role and to assume positions of power and responsibility. I do not think that one should condemn fantasies of domination on the grounds of their dislocation from reality. But we should examine what is wrong with the particular sort of fantasy in which men indulge when they read pornographic magazines.

In *The Sexuality of Men*, Andy Moye claims that the use to which the most heavily read porn is likely to be put is as material for masturbatory fantasy.[22] Moye makes the point that in masturbatory fantasy a man can control his sexual pleasure unaffected by performance anxiety or the sexual desire of the partner. This point about pornography controlling our sexuality is also emphasized by Richard Wollheim.[23] What can be wrong with using porn as material for masturbatory fantasy?

Let us imagine ourselves as readers of *Penthouse* in order to answer this question. In one photo a woman is smiling and relaxed; she stares erotically at her viewer, and yet, as Beverly Brown has emphasized, there is an 'everyday' quality about the image.[24] The viewer can lay aside, in his fantasy relations to this woman, the difficult, complex emotions he will experience in any actual relationship with a real woman, and concentrate on his own desire. He can picture the woman to whom he is relating as uncomplicatedly wanting him, her desire being to satisfy his. Thus, to use Richard Wollheim's analogy of the mind as a theatre, the viewer of the picture is, in his fantasy, an actor in a play that he has written, and she – the woman on the page – is there too, as his adoring lover, his woman, totally fixated upon him.

The woman represented on the pages of *Penthouse* is depicted as a subject who desires to lose her autonomy: she appears to want only to satisfy the desire of the man who gazes at her as he masturbates. What can be wrong, however, with fantasizing, treating a woman as an object and as a means if there is no connection between the fantasy and real life, and if she is depicted as wanting to be treated this way?

Wollheim's analogy of the mind as a theatre is again apt. In the theatre, he argues, there is (a) an internal dramatist, who makes up the characters and their actions; (b) an internal actor who represents to the reader for his benefit the actions he has made up as dramatist; and (c) an internal audience. After the fantasy performance, we, the individuals doing the fantasizing, are left with some reactions to our fantasy. The first link between the fantasy representation and the world outside is that the fantasy materials – the characters in the play and their actions – are drawn from real life. Even novels which appear to be furthest removed from the lives of those who wrote them (the works of Kafka, Lewis Carroll and of the contemporary feminist writer Marge Piercy, for example) have drawn on the real surroundings of their authors. And there is a particularly close connection in the case we are considering.

The fantasy relation between reader and text, in the case of a man reading *Playboy*, is more like the relation between consumer and a realist novel than that between reader and text of Kafka's *Metamorphosis*.

This is obviously not sufficient reason for us to condemn porn. The fantasy of the *Penthouse* reader may not involve any beliefs that real women behave as he imagines the woman on the page does. So what grounds are there for condemning porn?

As we have seen, the evidence for a causal connection between reading pornographic material and committing violent acts against women is inconclusive.[25] But even if there is not this causal connection, the fantasy does have a causal effect. Returning to

Wollheim's analogy: when the reader of the porn, as internal actor, performs his fantasy, he is left, as internal audience, in a state that simulates the state he would be in if he had actually had a relationship with a woman like the imagined one. The reader of *Penthouse* is left feeling pleasure. Although this may not lead to action like that in the representation, Wollheim argues, it acts as a lure to the formation of fresh dispositions to act, to the creation of fresh desires. In other words, the representation of the desire as pleasurably satisfied reinforces the desire to have a woman wholly concerned with his satisfaction. Thus pornographic representations are to be condemned because they reinforce the desire to treat people, and it is usually women, as objects. And while, as Susan Fagin[26] argues, the pleasures of fantasy are not limited to wanting the fantasy actually to occur, such desires involve treating women as means, and not as ends in themselves. The desires may involve coercing the woman into behaving in the way the man wants her to or construing the woman as wanting to behave in that way. Even if the desire is never satisfied except in fantasy, the man who constantly has such desires is to be condemned, for he is gaining satisfaction from a person whom he has divested of personhood and turned into a slave. Because his desires for these partial relationships are constantly satisfied he is less likely to seek out non-distorting, non-partial relationships in the rest of his life. Even though most porn involves fantasy, therefore, it is still open to condemnation. The individual consumer of porn can be blamed for divesting his fantasy object of personhood. Thus, Angela Carter, who describes porn as reinforcing the solipsistic concentration on the relationship with the self, is right in a way.[27] The reader of porn is focusing on himself. But Carter is also wrong: the *Playboy* reader is not concerned solely with himself; he is also relating to a fantasy image of a woman, and treating her in very much the way women have often been treated by men.

Porn and Collectives

There is an additional reason why the representation of relations between people in much pornography is wrong. It is, to state the obvious, mainly women who are depicted in pornography, and mainly men who are the consumers. In Chapter 4, I argued that there are circumstances in which it may be alright to curtail the autonomy of one individual in order to promote the interests of a group. In the case of pornography, the interests of the individual coalesce with those of the group. O and Justine are not just individuals, treated as means to the satisfaction of men's desires; they are also women. And women have, throughout history, been treated as women are treated in porn. Let us look at one example in which the treatment of women in porn reflects the way they have been generally viewed by men.

Porn, Women and Vision

In most pornography, women are objects constructed for the male gaze. Men look; women are looked at. In pornographic films, for instance, the darkened cinema gives the spectator the illusion of looking in on a private world. This enhances the pleasures of constructing another person as an object through sight, and subjecting their image to a controlling gaze. But it is not only in pornography that masculine vision assumes such prominence. As I mentioned in Chapter 3, visual metaphors have been used in epistemology throughout the western intellectual tradition. Feminists have argued that this is a masculine phenomenon.

Visual Metaphor in Epistemology

In the *Phaedrus*[28] Plato describes sight as 'the keenest of the senses'. He relates the predominance of vision to the pre-eminence of light as a medium of perception. The sun is the most important of the heavenly bodies, and vision is a process of matching like with like: the eye, like the sun, secretes light. But it is not just the real eye, in Plato, that sees. Knowledge of universals – of goodness, the form of the mountain or God – was conceived by analogy with the process of visual perception. Thus *nous* – thought, intellect – perceives universals, just as the eye sees particulars. Indeed Plato's theory of knowledge as recollection draws on this idea: individual souls once dwelt with the gods. There they enjoyed the same pure understanding of the cohesiveness of things as the gods once had. Yet, despite the actual absence of the senses from the process of knowledge, the phenomenon is described in visual terms. (The same phenomenon occurs in the Christian tradition, where God is described as the 'Light of Light'.) For Plato, then, proper knowledge is removed from the domain of the bodily senses, which can contaminate and distort. Yet he relies on visual imagery to describe the mental processes that take place. Vision, for him, is removed from the body, and functions outside time.

   Coming closer to the present, in the work of Descartes, this domination by the visual continues. In Dioptrics,[29] Descartes criticized the 'emission' theory, whereby light is emitted from the eye, yet he continued to use visual imagery: knowledge involves the mind, or the soul, 'seeing' its objects 'clearly' and 'distinctly'. For Descartes the knowing subject becomes the mind or the soul, and 'it' is quite distinct both from its objects of knowledge and from the body.

There is an obvious connection between the use of visual imagery and objectivity. In Descartes, as we have seen, the use of visual imagery continued alongside the severance of the 'I', the self, from the body, and the outside world. Nature – the object of knowledge – becomes distinct from the knowing subject, whose aim is to know it without being contaminated by it.

But the use of the visual is also connected with a conception of the self as unitary, whole and non-fragmented: Plato and Descartes both see the 'self', the 'subject', as a mental entity that perceives itself as well as other things clearly and distinctly. The ideal knower, for Plato, is someone who has freed him or herself from the contaminating influence of the body and the bodily senses, and who knows him or herself as he or she knows the form of the good. For Descartes, too, the self is a 'thinking' self, a self whose essence is transparently revealed to itself by means of the Cogito. The use of the type of visual imagery I have been describing – visual imagery which is removed from the bodily senses – lends itself to this conception of the subject.

What is the link between this body of thought and 'masculinity'? Several feminist philosophers have recently pointed out that the process of separating the subject from the object has often taken on gendered overtones. The connection is most explicit in the work of Francis Bacon, for whom the goal of science was explicitly described as that of 'conquering' and 'mastering' female nature: 'I am come in very truth leading you to Nature with all her children to find her to your service and make her your slave.'[30]

We come, then, to an additional reason for condemning pornography. O, Justine and the *Penthouse* models are women. They are representatives of a group that has, throughout history, and in a variety of ways, been treated as the object of a male gaze. In much Greek thought, as we have seen, women were represented as being closer to nature than men; their role in reproduction was meant to connect them to nature's fertility. Because they were closer to nature, it was possible to represent them as having whichever wants men desired them to have. In the Courtly Love tradition, the woman was put on a pedestal and represented as the object of desiring adoration and worship. We can conclude that men as a group are causally responsible for treating women as a group as though they were not autonomous.

The sense in which men as a group can be said to be responsible here is, of course, very different from the sense in which the jury in Chapter 3, is responsible for its actions. The group of men includes many different individuals, representatives of cultures, etc. I believe, however, that one could construct a number of different causal stories, connecting different groups of men back to the original occasions when individual men carried out acts of objectifying women. All men would be connected, in some way, in this picture. Pornography reinforces the power of men as a group. In this way, men as a group can be blamed for the way women are treated in porn. They are responsible for eroticizing women's oppression.

Women's Pornography

There is one significant fact that I have so far left out of the picture: the role of women pornographers. *The Story of O* was apparently written by a woman, Pauline Reage. And even if the name is a pseudonym, plenty of Mills and Boon romances are authored by women. How does this affect the position? The heroines of the romances, like O and Justine, are depicted as wanting nothing so much as to satisfy their men's desire. In *Unguarded Moment* Alix wants to satisfy Liam's wants; she wants him to want her. In this respect Alix is just like O. The extent of O's loss of selfhood and subjectivity is more extreme, yet the phenomenon is the same. I said earlier in this chapter, that no rational person, in the absence of constraints, would choose to be tortured. It is also true, up to a point, that no rational person, in the absence of constraints, would choose to be treated as not autonomous. It is unlikely that any woman, if she had alternative outlets for her fantasies, would choose the role of a Mills and Boon heroine. Is the reader of the romantic fiction, therefore, not to be condemned for concurring in her own subordination? Perhaps to a certain extent she is, and yet there are several factors that work against this conclusion.

In Chapter 4 I argued that one person can be held responsible, and blamed, for the actions of another. A familiar example is the case of a parent and child. We could say, in the case in point, that if we were to attribute blame, then we ought not to blame the reader of the Mills and Boon novel, but the person, or people, responsible for propagating the values she has internalized. This would be men as a group. But it is also true that the position of the female reader of romantic fiction is not so clear-cut as that of the male consumer of *Penthouse*. The latter is clearly fantasizing about treating the woman on its pages as a means. The Mills and Boon reader may be doing many other things (learning English, one said, seeking privacy) in addition to gaining erotic pleasure. The act of reading a romantic fiction novel can be seen as a strong affirmation of independence against the passivity and self-destruction of depression, as well as behaviour perpetuating the passive, subjective role. The structure of the romantic fiction text is identical to porn magazines in so far as it involves the fantasy depiction of a woman in the role of means to the satisfaction of another's desire. But the relation between reader and text is different and more complicated. Women's porn is a reflection of the patriarchal values of male porn, but its readers are not so straightforwardly open to condemnation as their male counterparts.

Pornography, Individualism and Feminism

Pornography, and the patriarchal values it embodies, is an individualist pursuit. Like the units of moral and methodological individualism, the female objects of the male pornographic magazines and films are stripped of individuating features. Moral individualist theory refers to people divested of all their relevant moral interests: they are said to be equal in respect of being the possessors of interests and the bearers of rights. The male consumers and the female objects in porn are equal too, in respect of their being the possessors of sexual desire. Nothing else matters. And just as liberal rights theorists advocating a right to property are introducing an actual inequality into the picture, so too are pornographers papering over an actual inequality: men are the subjects of desire, women are its objects. This is true both for male and for female pornography.

Pornography rests on liberal individualist values.[31] It relies on assumptions about the 'freedoms', the 'rights' of the producer and consumer of the material. Both are seen as abstract individuals. The continued existence of pornography depends on these individualistic presuppositions. If the facts of gender were brought into the picture, the justification for the continued dissemination of pornography would be undermined. 'The male right to treat women as means' does not have the high moral tone of 'the individual right to disseminate/read material as he or she wishes.'

Additionally, pornography depends upon 'self-directed' values – individualistic ones – as opposed to the collectivist 'other-directed' qualities. Sir Stephen and the man reading *Penthouse* are thinking not of others, but of themselves. Their desires and behaviour towards the woman are not motivated by care and concern for her; rather they derive from feelings the men project on to her. Thus their 'other-directed' behaviour is like that of the arch individualist in the Kantian/Rawlsean tradition, for whom thinking of the other means 'putting oneself in the other's shoes'. This is in contrast to a collectivist viewpoint, where thinking of the other means allowing one's horizon to merge with theirs.

De Sade and Individualism

The 'greatest' pornographer of all, the Marquis de Sade, was a classic individualist. According to the philosopher Adorno: 'The work of the Marquis de Sade portrays "understanding without the guidance of another person"; that is the bourgeois individual freed from tutelage.'[32]

De Sade was a true Enlightenment thinker. His heroine Juliette scorns public opinion, reputation, conventions and prejudices. Instead, she follows her reason. Her own 'new conscience' which 'stands aloof from superstition and vulgar claptrap'[33] is her guide. Her teacher Mme Delbene leads her along nature's path by logical argument and demonstration. Mme Delbene pursues the views of the English corpuscularians, who influenced the French writers for the *Encyclopédie*, to their logical conclusions. God is an 'abominable Ghost'[34] whose existence cannot be demonstrated. The fantasy that there is a God 'has its origins in nothing but the mind's limitations.'[35] As for Christ, Mme Delbene again uses typical Enlightenment reasoning: 'I persevere in my quest for some solid evidence of him, I summon reason to my end, and lest it deceive me, I subject reason itself to analysis.'[36] Mme Delbene uses Cartesian or Kantian reasoning and reaches a conclusion that Descartes or Kant perhaps ought to have reached, atheism. 'Reason is the test against which we submit forth.'[37] And she uses Lockean reasoning to suggest that God and the soul exist only in the minds of the deluded. She disposes of the first-cause argument for God's existence and compares God to a vampire (one caused blood to be spilt; the other drank blood): both are 'figments of a disordered imagination.'[38]

Through the figure of Mme Delbene, de Sade shows himself to be a typical Enlightenment individualist. The person is self-sufficient; there can be no reliance on tradition, authority, prejudice or religion. The self is the unit of moral regard, the possessor of interests, and the bearer of rights; interests become solely the satisfaction of needs and desires, and rights become the right to pleasure in excess.

Not for de Sade are the classic liberal constraints on individual action. Mill's 'harm condition' is far from his purview. He is the pure liberal individualist. For him, others exist purely as means to the satisfaction of his desires. As I pointed out earlier, when I referred to Battaille's writings on de Sade and in the chapter on Kappeler, this pure liberal individualism is self-refuting. In destroying others, de Sade is destroying himself. Yet de Sade illustrates, in perfect form, the interconnection between 'the pornographer' and the liberal individualist.

De Sade shares certain values with Nietzsche. Both denigrate Christian values as the 'ethic' of the weak and downtrodden; both extol the self, untrammelled by any extraneous influences. Nietzsche proclaimed: 'The weak and unsuccessful must perish; this is the first proposition of our philanthropy.'[39] Adorno compares Nietzsche with de Sade, who said: 'Christianity, singularly desirous of subjugating tyrants and forcing them to acknowledge the doctrine of brotherhood ... takes up the role of the weak; it represents them and has to speak and sound like them ...'[40] I leave the reader to draw their own conclusions.

De Sade is an extreme liberal individualist. Yet he shares with Bernard Williams et al. the view that the producer of porn is an individual with a right to do as he pleases. For a collectivist, by contrast, who takes class into consideration, the right in question is that of the producer's right to exploit the consumers in order to make a profit.

Looking at things from the two different collectivist viewpoints – one taking gender into account, the other considering class – we arrive at a very different picture from the individualist one. As a (likely) member of the working class the male consumer of porn is exploited; as a man, he is an oppressor. The female shareholder in Mills and Boon is an oppressor, although as a woman she is treated as a means.

The individualist, therefore, is distorting the picture by failing to bring the facts of gender and class to the fore. But those radical feminists who, like Dworkin, Griffin and Kappeler, describe porn as a 'male' preserve with women straightforwardly in the position of the oppressed group, also mislead. Because there is porn for women, women are not always in the subjugated position. Sometimes men, as members of the working class, are in this position. When the facts of race are brought in, the position is further complicated. If the woman in *Penthouse* is black, she is subjugated not just as a woman, but also as a black person, as a member of a group that historically has been oppressed.

Conclusion

We have found three reasons for criticizing porn. First of all, the individual male consumer of a pornographic magazine can be blamed for treating his fantasy object as a slave, as a means to the satisfaction of his desires. Secondly, men, collectively, can be blamed for the loss of autonomy, in general, and in porn in particular, of women as a group. And thirdly, one can condemn the individualist values that underlie the justification for pornography.

Conclusion

What conclusions can we draw? The tactics used against pornography by feminists over the last twenty years have been many and varied. Imaginative and provocative attempts have been made to demonstrate the point that pornography degrades and 'objectifies' women. One example of a consciousness-raising tactic of this kind was the demonstration on 7 February, 1969 by a group of American women who invaded a room where the manager of *Playboy*'s college promotions department was expounding the magazine's philosophy to about 75 college students. The women distributed literature and removed their clothes.[1] The 'nude-in' received national press coverage, and contributed to raising awareness of the position of women in pornography.

Pickets, sit-ins, leafleting and lobbying have all been useful tactics to promote views about particular pornographic publications. Picketing and leafleting cinemas showing the horrific movie *Snuff*, which involved the ritual and sadistic butchering of a young woman for sexual pleasure, resulted both in the film being removed from circulation, and, one hopes, in the increased awareness of the immorality of connecting sex and murder. Similarly successful campaigns have been waged against other pornographic films, and nowadays one finds many a man inveighing against the exploitation of women in a film like *Emmanuelle*, for instance.

There is one sort of campaigning against pornography, however, that I would describe as inappropriate and liable to be counterproductive. As we saw in Chapter 5, feminists in the USA, following Andrea Dworkin and Catherine McKinnon, have recommended banning pornography. They have not been the only ones to have suggested this tactic. WAVAW feminists in the UK have advocated censorship:

> To launch an attack on porn we have to make a stand, to say that it is not the god-given right of any ruling group with money and power to plaster the environment with their sadistic, demoralising and

degrading view of a less powerful section of society. If this is to advocate censorship, then that is what we must do.[2]

Andrea Dworkin, in an article (which *The Times* did not publish) written in response to a *New York Times* editorial applauding the First Amendment's protection of the 'freedom' of expression, had this to say:

> The Constitution of the United States was written exclusively by white men who owned land ... The Bill of Rights was never intended to protect the civil or sexual rights of women and it has not, except occasionally by accident ... The government in all its aspects – legislative, executive, judicial, enforcement – has been composed almost exclusively of men. Both law and pornography express male contempt for women.

Again we see Dworkin downplaying the role of class and race: what, one wonders, does she believe is the connection between being white and owning land with adopting a sympathetic attitude towards pornographers and pornography? How can she move from saying that the law was written by white landowning men to the view that it expresses a specifically male contempt for women? Are non-white, non-landowning men also complicit in the law's contempt for women, even though the law is regularly used against them? And finally, why should the fact that the law was drawn up by white landowning men have any bearing at all on its function and role today? It is possible that there might be no connection between the two. Some white liberals in South Africa, for example, have attempted to use their white liberal privileges to promote views that run contrary to the apartheid of the South African state. One wonders, too, what relevance these views have to Dworkin's advocacy of a ban on porn. (One might also wonder what Dworkin would say about those women – the Prime Minister of the UK, for example – who have been instrumental in the drafting of the constitutions of their country, and whether she believes that if any government had been entirely composed of women, it would necessarily have enacted anti-porn legislation. The pro-*Penthouse*, *Playboy*, etc., views of many women lead me to doubt this.)

What other arguments are used in favour of banning porn? One group of feminists justifies censorship along these lines:

> We had always regarded freedom of speech as a given and

unquestionable right, and we found ourselves contradicting this freedom for pornographers. Our thinking was clarified somewhat when we considered the denial of free speech to women and the exclusion of women's voices in all popular culture.[3]

Does a wrong committed elsewhere constitute grounds for carrying it out once more? In Chapter 1 we saw that it did not; 'two wrongs do not make a right', to use the proverb.

The British WAVAW feminists are less concerned with rights and more concerned with the damage done by porn. 'We must demand that porn be prohibited on the grounds it is an "incitement to sexual hatred", in fact a clear incitement to rape and murder', they say, 'as well as to the general inferiorisation of women.'[4] Again, I have argued that a causal connection between porn and rape is unproven. Furthermore, following Skillen's view, we might conjecture that suppressing a racist or fascist (or pornographic) viewpoint might have precisely the consequence of strengthening it. This, we saw, was indeed what happened with the British government's attempt to ban Peter Wright's *Spycatcher*, a book about the British secret service.

There are other reasons, too, for not banning porn.[5] As Marianne Valverde has pointed out, it is all too easy for feminist attempts to eliminate an outrage perpetrated against women to turn into attacks on them. She argues that Toronto mayor Art Eggleton, in a submission to the Canadian government's Fraser Commission on Pornography and Prostitution of February 1984, 'cynically used women's anger about porn in order to further his own law and order interests. He promised an all-out crackdown not just on pornography but on what he called "the double-headed beast of pornography and prostitution."'[6] Robin Morgan argues that 'a phallocentric culture is more likely to begin its censorship purges with books on pelvic self-examination for women.'[7] Although I demur at Morgan's expression 'phallocentric culture', her point is well made.

The crackdown on pornography and prostitution is reminiscent of the treatment of prostitutes in nineteenth-century Britain. But it also reminds one of the differential treatment that has been meted out to representatives of marginal groups relative to those that are not marginal. Gay bookshops in the UK have recently been raided because they sell books advocating homosexuality. Violent, sadistic books, on the other hand, are readily available in non-gay bookshops.

My point is this: unless the lawyers, judges and juries who are responsible for implementing the law are educated not to discriminate against minority and oppressed groups in society, any law which may be designed by its protagonists to protect those groups is liable to be used against them. This point is again illustrated by Valverde, who says that 'the Toronto police recently confiscated a feminist art exhibit displayed in a bookstore window and charged the artists with obscenity.'[8]

Finally, the legal approach to pornography assumes that images and texts have meanings that are independent of the context of their production and use. But as we have seen, this is not the case. In Gregory Peck's film *The Male Nude*, the hero refers to men's use of *National Geographic* as a vehicle for masturbatory fantasy. As we have seen, Valverde describes how the soft-core porn magazine *Forum* appropriated the novel written by lesbian ex-nuns and published by a feminist press.[9] Both the meaning given to the story, and the use to which it was put, would have been very different in the two contexts. A legal approach to pornography would obscure these differences because it assumes that a court can decide, simply by examining a particular representation, whether it is pornographic.[10]

Banning porn would not end the treatment of women as a means of satisfying male desires or their role as objects for the male gaze. This happens in many places outside porn. Porn is just one case – a graphic one perhaps – illustrating the more general phenomenon of male power.

Only the removal of male power more generally would eliminate the treatment of women as means. But pornography is also a class question. The elimination of male power is necessary, but not sufficient, for getting rid of the ills of porn. Elimination of class, and its attendant inequalities, is also necessary.

These are grandiose, high-sounding goals. Not only do they depend on a type of human interaction that is idealistic and utopian – of people cooperating equally without exploiting one another – but they are also premised on the unrealistic conception of people as whole, unitary, rational beings. However idealistic it may be, however, it is important that this ideal function as a goal and a standard. The view that women are treated wholly as objects, wholly as means, is an exaggeration. But it is one which enables us to see how closely porn approaches it: O is very like it; Justine perhaps less so. The magnification enables us to criticize those aspects of our actual behaviour that approach it. Very few actual men are like Sir Stephen, but we can criticize behaviour in individual men whenever it approaches his. Similarly, behaviour which approaches the ideal can be applauded.

We can confidently say that few people would be whole-heartedly criticized or applauded. Most people are like Sue in *Jude the Obscure*, with contradictory feelings and desires. A feminist emphasis on care and concern for others, and respect for the autonomy of other people, would encourage people like Sue to shun the position of object and to assume a more independent perspective. It is unlikely, however, that anyone will ever be wholly as the ideal assumes, because the whole, unitary rational self is ultimately unattainable.

We should none the less strive for a non-patriarchal, non-class divided world as an ideal towards which our behaviour might approximate. Even if it is not achievable, the ideal is an important one.

Notes

Introduction

1. See, for example, Anthony Burgess, 'What is Pornography?' in Douglas A. Hughes (ed.), *Perspectives on Pornography* (New York: Macmillan, 1970).
2. Kenneth Tynan, 'Dirty Books Can Stay' in ibid., pp. 109–21.
3. See Judith R. Walkowitz, *Prostitution and Victorian Society: Women, Class and the State* (London: Cambridge University Press, 1980).

Chapter 1: The Liberal Position: Freedom of Speech

1. Bernard Williams et al. *Report of the Committee on Obscenity and Film Censorship* in the House of Commons Command Papers, No. 7772, 1979 (hereafter, Williams Report). For a discussion of some of the issues raised in the report, see Anthony Skillen, 'Offences Ranked: the Williams Report on Obscenity', *Philosophy*, 57 (1982) pp. 237–45. See also Beverly Brown, 'Private Faces in Public Places' in *Ideology and Consciousness*, No. 7 (Autumn 1980) pp. 3–16.
2. Williams Report, para 5.24, p. 56.
3. Ibid., p. 56.
4. Ibid., para 5.7, p. 51.
5. Ibid., para 5.421, p. 56.
6. Ibid., para 5.24, p. 56.
7. *New York Times*, 14 January 1988.
8. Ibid.
9. Roy Edgley, 'Freedom of Speech and Academic Freedom', *Radical Philosophy*, No. 10 (Spring 1975) p. 10.
10. Ibid., p. 12.
11. Karl Popper, *The Open Society and its Enemies*, Vol. 1 (London: Routledge, 1962) p. 266.
12. Anthony Skillen, 'Freedom of Speech' in Keith Graham (ed.), *Contemporary Political Philosophy*, (Cambridge: Cambridge University Press, 1982) p. 141.
13. Popper, *The Open Society*, p. 265.
14. Skillen, 'Freedom of Speech', p. 142.

15. See Jonathan Glover, *Causing Death and Saving Lives* (Harmondsworth: Penguin, 1974), Chapter 7;   J. Bennett, 'Morality and Consequences' in McMurrin (ed.) *The Lectures on Human Values* (Cambridge: Cambridge University Press, 1981) Chapter 5.

16. J.L. Austin, *How To Do Things with Words* (Oxford: Oxford University Press, 1962).

17. Paul Goodman, 'Pornography, Art and Censorship' in Douglas A. Hughes (ed.), *Perspectives on Pornography* (New York: Macmillan, 1970).

18. Woolsey, quoted in ibid., p. 49.

19. Jacques Derrida, *Of Grammatology*, trans. Guyatri Spivak, (Baltimore: Johns Hopkins University Press, 1976).

20. Sir Keith Joseph in *The Times*, 4 December 1974.

21. Isaiah Berlin, 'Two Concepts of Liberty' in *Four Essays on Liberty* (Oxford: Clarendon Press, 1969) p. 136.

22. David D. Raphael, *Problems of Political Philosophy* (London: Macmillan, 1969).

23. Richard Lindley, *Autonomy* (Basingstoke: Macmillan, 1986) p. 95.

24. Keith Graham, *The Battle of Democracy* (Brighton: Wheatsheaf, 1986) p. 47.

25. Edgley, 'Freedom of Speech', p. 12.

26. See Bert Kutchinsky, 'Obscenity and Pornography, Behavioural Aspects' in Sandford H. Kadish et al. (eds) *Encyclopedia of Crime and Justice*, Vol. 3 (New York: Macmillan, Free Press, 1983) note 4.

27. Quoted in David Hebditch and Nick Anning, *Porn Gold, Inside the Pornography Business* (London and Boston: Faber & Faber, 1986) p. 90.

28. Ibid., p. 95.

29. Ibid., p. 89.

30. Ibid., p. 106.

31. See Williams Report, pp. 61–86.

32. I am deliberately referring to women here because they are the people who are usually in this position. But the argument of this chapter could apply equally to men.

33. See Lindley, *Autonomy*, for this kind of argument in relation to autonomy.

34. Karl Marx, 'On the Jewish Question', in Karl Marx, *Early Writings*, ed. L. Colletti (Harmondsworth: Penguin, 1975) p. 229.

Chapter 2: The Liberal Position: The Public and the Private

1. Williams Report, p. 96.

2. Ibid., para 7.4, p. 96.

3. Ibid., para 9.2, p. 112.

4. In *Private Faces* Beverly Brown argues that the Williams Report adopts the strategy of the Wolfenden Report (Report of the Committee on Homosexual Offences and Prostitutes), Chair, John Wolfenden (New York: Lancer Books) which involves a shrinkage of legislative control over personal conduct combined with a more rigorous policing of the cordon representing the public domain.
5. Williams Report, para 9.10, p. 115.
6. Ibid., para 9.14, p. 117.
7. Ibid., para 7.6, p. 97.
8. Ernest Baker (ed.), *The Politics of Aristotle* (Oxford: Oxford University Press, 1962) pp. 4,5.
9. T. Hobbes, *Leviathan*, ed. W.G. Podgson Smith (Oxford: Oxford University Press, 1965) p. 154.
10. Ibid., pp. 154, 157.
11. J.S. Mill, 'On Marriage and Divorce' in Mill and Taylor, *Essays on Sex Equality*, quoted in Richard W. Krouse: 'Patriarchal Liberalism and Beyond' in Jean Elshtain (ed.), *The Family in Political Thought* (Brighton: Harvester Press, 1982) p. 164.
12. Krouse, ibid., p. 164.
13. Carol Gould, 'Private Rights and Public Virtues: Women, The Family and Democracy' in C. Gould (ed.), *Beyond Domination: New Perspectives on Women and Philosophy* (New Jersey: Rowman & Allenheld, 1984) p. 7.
14. Ibid., p. 7.
15. See, for example, Samuel Warren and Louis Brandeis, 'The Right to Privacy', *Harvard Law Review*, 4 (1980) pp. 203–7.
16. Isaiah Berlin, 'Two Concepts of Liberty', p. 92.
17. John Stuart Mill, *On Liberty* (London: Pelican, 1974) p. 69.
18. Plato, *The Republic*, trans. Allen Bloom (New York: Basic Books, 1968) p. 420b.
19. Berlin, 'Two Concepts of Liberty', p. 95.
20. Jean Elshtain, 'Introduction: Towards a Theory of the Family and Politics' in Jean Elshtain (ed.), *The Family in Political Thought* (Brighton: Harvester, 1982).

Chapter 3: Individualism

1. See K.W. Smart, 'Individualism in the Mid-19th Century (1826–1860)' *Journal of the History of Ideas*, 23 (1962) pp. 77–90; see also Stephen Lukes, *Individualism* (Oxford: Oxford University Press, 1973) and Hans Georg Gadamer, *Truth and Method* (London: Sheed & Ward, 1979).
2. Hans Georg Gadamer, *Truth and Method* (London: Sheed & Ward, 1981).
3. Bernard Williams, 'The Certainty of the Cogito', in Willis Doney

(ed.), *Descartes* (New York: Garden City, 1967).

4. Rene Descartes, 'Third Meditation' in *Descartes' Philosophical Writings*, trans. and ed. by Elizabeth Anscombe and Peter Geach (London: Nelson's University Paperback, 1954).

5. See Stephen Lukes, *Individualism*, Chapter 2.

6. See, for instance, Carol Gilligan, 'Remapping the Moral Domain' in Thomas Heller, Martin Sosna and David Welbury (eds), *Reconstructing Individualism* (Stanford: Stanford University Press, 1986) pp. 237–52.

7. Ibid., p. 240.

8. C.B. Macpherson, *The Political Theory of Possessive Individualism, Hobbes to Locke* (Oxford: Oxford University Press, 1962).

9. John Rawls, *A Theory of Justice* (Oxford: Oxford University Press, 1971).

10. Keith Graham, *The Battle of Democracy*, p. 104.

11. See H.G. Gadamer, *Truth and Method*.

12. John Rawls, *Justice*, p. 60.

13. Ibid., p. 61.

14. Ibid., p. 440.

15. Luce Irigaray, *Speculum of the Other Woman*, trans. Gillian C. Gill (New York: Cornell University Press, 1985).

16. Ibid., pp. 168–69.

17. Ibid., p. 183.

18. Margaret Walters, *The Nude Male* (New York and London: Paddington Press, 1978) p. 17.

19. Rosemary Tong, 'Feminism, Pornography and Censorship', *Social Theory and Practice*, para. 8, No. 1, 4 (Spring 1982).

20. Eva Fox Kittay, 'Porn and the Erotics of Domination' in Carol Gould (ed.), *Beyond Domination: New Perspectives on Woman and Philosophy* (New York: Rowman & Allenheld, 1984) p. 166.

Chapter 4: Autonomy

1. Nancy Chodorow 'Towards a Relational Individualism: the Mediation of Self Through Psychoanalysis', in Thomas Heller (ed.) *Reconstructing Individualism*.

2. Carol Gilligan, 'Remapping the Moral Domain' in Heller (ed.), ibid.

3. Immanuel Kant, 'Groundwork to the Metaphysic of Morals' (1785) in H. J. Paen (ed.), *The Moral Law* (London: Hutchinson, 1948).

4. Harry Frankfurt, 'Freedom of the Will and the Concept of a Person', *Journal of Philosophy*, Vol. 68 (1971) p. 8.

5. Arthur Kulfik, 'The Independence of Autonomy', *Philosophy and Public Affairs*, Vol. 13, No. 4 (Fall 1984) p. 283.

6. See Keith Graham, 'Democracy and the Autonomous Moral Agent' in

Keith Graham (ed.), *Contemporary Political Philosophy*.
7. See Richard Lindley, *Autonomy*.
8. Ibid., p. 78.
9. Ibid., pp. 74–86.
10. Bernard Williams, *Moral Luck* (Cambridge: Cambridge University Press, 1982).

Chapter 5: Dworkin: Male Power and Violence

1. See the complete transcript of the public hearings or ordinances to add pornography as discrimination, Minneapolis City Council, Government Operations Committee, 12 and 13 December 1983, in *Pornography and Sexual Violence: Evidence of the Links* (London: Everywoman Press, 1988).
2. Andrea Dworkin, *Pornography: Men Possessing Women* (London: The Women's Press, 1981) p. 1.
3. Ibid., p .13.
4. Ibid., p. 4.
5. Ibid., pp. 15–16.
6. Ibid., p. 15.
7. Ibid., pp. 15–16.
8. Ibid., p. 17.
9. Ibid., p. 18.
10. Ibid., p. 19.
11. Ibid., p. 15.
12. Ibid., pp. 20–1.
13. Ibid., p. 23.
14. Ibid., p. 25.
15. Ibid., p. 24.
16. Ibid., p. 25.
17. Ibid., pp. 25–6.
18. It is interesting that Dworkin picks this particular piece of pornography and not, as Alan Soble argues, the much more commonplace pornographic 'beaver' – photos of women exhibiting their genitals. (See Alan Soble, *Pornography* [New Haven and London: Yale University Press, 1986], p. 89.) Ruby Rich, giving an analysis of the 'anti-porn' film says this: 'the anti-porn film is an acceptable replacement for porn itself, a kind of snuff movie for an anti-snuff crowd. In this version, outrage against replaces pleasure in, but the object of the preposition remains the same ... The question, though, is whether this outcry becomes itself a hand maiden to titillation, whether this alleged look of horror is not perhaps a most sophisticated form of voyeurism?' (Ruby Rich, 'Anti-Porn, Hard World', *Feminist Review* [Spring 1983], pp. 56–67). Might not

Dworkin's predilection for particularly nasty pieces of porn need explaining too?

19. Sheila Jeffreys, 'Pornography', paper written for London Regional Revolutionary Feminist Conference, February 1978.

20. Irene Diamond, 'Pornography and Repression. A Reconsideration of "Who" and "What"' in Laura Lederer (ed.), *Take Back the Night: Women on Pornography* (New York: Bantam Books, 1980).

21. Jeffreys, 'Pornography'.

22. Dusty Rhodes and Sandra McNeill (eds), *Women Against Violence Against Women* (London: Only Women Press, 1981).

23. Kate Millett, *Sexual Politics* (London: Virago, 1972), p. 25.

24. Carol Smart and B. Smart (eds), *Women, Sexuality and Social Control* (London: Routledge, 1978) p. 100.

25. Dworkin, *Pornography*, p. 25.

26. Wendy Hollway, quoting a feminist friend of hers, in 'Heterosexual Sex: Power and Desire for the Other' in Sue Cartledge and Joanne Ryan (eds), *Sex and Love* (London: The Women's Press, 1983) p. 128.

27. Sue Cartledge, describing her own feelings, in 'Duty and Desire: Creating a Feminist Morality' in ibid., p. 172.

28. Ellen Willis, 'Feminism, Moralism and Pornography' in Ann Snitow, Christine Stansell and Sharon Thompson (eds), *Desire: The Politics of Sexuality* (London: Virago, 1983) p. 86.

29. Dusty Rhodes and Sandra McNeill, *Women Against Violence Against Women*.

30. Caroline Ramazanoglu, 'Sex and Violence in Academic Life, You Can't Keep a Good Woman Down' in Jalna Hanmer and Mary Maynard (eds), *Women, Violence and Social Control* (London: Macmillan, 1987).

31. Ibid., p. 64.

32. Dale Spender, *Man Made Language* (London: Routledge, 1980), and Alison Assiter, 'Did Man Make Language?', *Radical Philosophy*, No. 34, (1984).

33. D. Rhodes et al., *Women Against Violence Against Women*, pp. 253–5.

34. Ibid., p. 254.

35. Ruth Bleier, *Science and Gender* (New York: Pergamon Press, 1984).

36. See Angela Davies, *Women, Race and Class* (London: The Women's Press, 1981).

37. See Lawrence Rosenfeld, 'Politics and Pornography', *Quarterly Journal of Speech*, 59 (1973) pp. 413–22.

38. David Chute, 'Dirty Pillow Talk', *Boston Phoenix*, 23 September 1980.

39. See Philip Roth, *Portnoy's Complaint*.

40. Alan Soble, *Pornography*.

41. Andy Moye, 'Pornography' in A. Metcalf and Martin Humphreys

(eds), *The Sexuality of Men* (London: Pluto Press, 1985).

42. See, for example, Anne Phillips, *Divided Loyalties* (London: Virago, 1987).

43. Geoffrey Gorer, 'The Uses of Porn' in *The Danger of Equality* (New York: Weybright & Talley, 1966) pp. 217–31.

44. Susan Griffin, *Pornography and Silence* (London: The Women's Press, 1981).

45. In Catherine Itzin, 'The Campaign Trail Starts Here', *Guardian*, 2 February 1988, p. 22.

46. Sally Wagner, 'Porn and the Sexual Revolution: the Backlash of S-M' in R. Linden et al. (eds) *Against Sado-Masochism, a Radical Feminist Analysis* (East Palo Alto: Frog in the Wall, 1982).

47. Kathleen Barry, *Female Sexual Slavery* (New York and London: New York University Press, 1984) p. 217.

48. David Hebditch and Dick Anning, *Porn Gold: Inside the Pornography Business* (London: Faber & Faber, 1988) p. 139.

49. Ibid., p. 47.

50. Ibid., p. 47.

51. Marianne Valverde, *Sex, Power and Pleasure* (Toronto: The Women's Press, 1985).

52. Gayle Rubin, quoted in Deirdre English, Amber Hollingsborough and Gayle Rubin, 'Talking Sex: A Conversation on Sexuality and Feminism', *Feminist Review* No. 11 (1982), p. 48.

53. In D. Rhodes et al., *Women Against Violence Against Women*, p. 16.

54. Anthony Burgess, 'What is Pornography?' in Douglas A. Hughes (ed.) *Perspectives on Pornography* (New York: Macmillan, 1970).

55. Sylvia Levine and Joseph Koerig (eds), *Why Men Rape* (London: W. H. Allen, 1982) p. 1.

56. Bert Kutchinsky, 'The Effect of Easy Availability of Porn on the Incidence of Sex Crimes: The Danish Experience', *Journal of Social Issues*, Vol. XXIX, No. 5 (June 1973) pp. 165–81.

57. Thelma McCormack, 'Machismo in Media Research: A Critical Review of Research on Violence and Porn', *Social Problems*, Vol. XXV, No. 5 (June 1978) pp. 552–4.

58. Seymour Fishback and Neal Malamuth, 'Sex and Aggression: Proving the Link', *Psychology Today*, Vol. XII, No. 6 (1978).

59. Williams Report.

60. Dworkin, *Pornography*, p. 200.

61. Ibid., p. 162.

Chapter 6: Dworkin: The Self

1. Andrea Dworkin, *Intercourse* (London: Secker & Warburg, 1987) p. 128.

2. Friedrich Nietzsche, *Untimely Meditations* (Cambridge: Cambridge

University Press, 1983).

3. Friedrich Nietzsche, *Twilight of the Idols and the Antichrist*, trans. R.J. Hollingdale (Harmondsworth: Penguin, 1968) p. 92.
4. Ibid., p. 96.
5. Ibid., p. 92.
6. Dworkin, *Intercourse*, p. 85.
7. Ibid., p. 85.
8. Nietzsche, *Twilight*, p. 90.
9. Nietzsche, *On the Genealogy of Morals*, trans. W. Kaufmann (New York: Vintage Books, 1969) p. 36.
10. 'Resentment' may be a misleading translation of this word. (See Kaufmann's introduction to the *Genealogy*, pp. 5–9, for a discussion of the sense.)
11. Ibid., p. 19.
12. Ibid., p. 39.
13. Nietzsche, *The Revolt of the Masses* (Madrid, 1930) Chapter 1.
14. Ibid., Chapter 2.
15. Dworkin, *Intercourse*, p. 96.
16. Dworkin, *Intercourse*, p. 114.
17. Dworkin, *Right-Wing Women* (London: The Women's Press, 1982) p. 40.
18. See Jean Baker Miller, *Towards a New Psychology of Women* (Harmondsworth: Pelican, 1978).
19. Simone de Beauvoir, *The Second Sex* (Toronto: Bantam Books, 1964).
20. Ibid., p. 727.
21. Ibid., p. 727.
22. Mary Daly, *Gyn/Ecology: The Metaethics of Radical Feminism* (London: The Women's Press, 1979).
23. Judith Okely, *Simone de Beauvoir* (London: Virago, 1986).
24. Ibid., p. 71.
25. Lynn Segal, *Is the Future Female?* (London: Virago, 1987).
26. Ibid., p. 214.
27. Ibid., p. 213
28. Cynthia Cockburn, *Brothers, Male Dominance and Technological Change* (London: Pluto Press, 1983).
29. D.H. Lawrence, *Sons and Lovers* (Harmondsworth: Penguin, 1987).
30. Dworkin, *Intercourse*, p. 68.
31. Ibid., p. 114.
32. Ibid., p. 5.
33. Angela V. John, *By the Sweat of their Brow: Women Workers at Victorian Coal Mines* (London: Croom Helm, 1980).
34. Dworkin, *Intercourse*, p. 114.
35. Jacques Lacan, *Ecrits* (London: Tavistock, 1977).

36. Ibid., p. 168.
37. Jacques Derrida, *Of Grammatology.*
38. Lynn Segal, 'Sensual Uncertainty or Why the Clitoris is not Enough' in Sue Cartledge and Joanna Ryan (eds), *Sex and Love* (London: The Women's Press, 1983).
39. Sigmund Freud, *Introductory Lectures on Psychoanalysis* (Harmondsworth: Penguin, 1973), quoted in Jean Grimshaw, 'Autonomy and Identity in Feminist Thinking' in Morwenna Griffiths and Margaret Whitford (eds), *Feminist Perspectives in Philosophy* (London: Macmillan, 1988), p. 101.
40. Ibid., p. 101.
41. Sigmund Freud, 'On the Sexual Theories of Children' in S. Freud, *On Sexuality* (Harmondsworth: Penguin, 1986) p. 188.
42. Thomas Hardy, *Jude the Obscure* (Harmondsworth: Penguin, 1978).
43. Quoted in Thomas Hardy's 1912 preface to *Jude the Obscure.*
44. Preface to *Jude the Obscure.*
45. Ibid., p. 246.
46. Ibid., p. 246.
47. Ibid., p. 239.
48. J.S. Mill, *On the Subjection of Women* (London: Virago, 1983).

Chapter 7: The Freudian Griffin

1. Susan Griffin, *Pornography and Silence* (London: The Women's Press, 1981) p. 1.
2. Ibid., p. 2.
3. Ibid., p. 57.
4. Ibid., p. 59.
5. Ibid., p. 87.
6. Ibid., p. 85.
7. Ibid., p. 83.
8. Marianne Valverde, 'Pornography' in *No Safe Place, Violence Against Women and Children*, ed. Connie Gubermann and Margie Wolfe (Toronto: Women's Press Issues, 1985) p. 142.
9. Susanne Kappeler, *The Pornography of Representation* (Cambridge: Polity Press, 1986) pp. 52–3.
10. Griffin, *Pornography*, p. 20.
11. Ibid., p. 68.
12. Ibid., p. 60.
13. Ibid., p. 60.
14. Ibid., p. 61.
15. Wendy Hollway, 'Heterosexual Sex: Power and Desire for the Other' in Joanna Ryan and Sue Cartledge (eds), *Sex and Love*, p. 12.
16. Griffin, *Pornography*, p. 15.

17. De Sade, *Philosophy in the Bedroom*, quoted in Griffin, ibid., p. 69.
18. Valverde, 'Pornography', p. 139.
19. Levine and Koerig (eds), *Why Men Rape*.
20. Linda Imray and Audrey Middleton, 'Public and Private: Marking the Boundaries' in Eva Gamarnikow, David Morgan, June Purvis and Daphne Taylorson (eds), *The Public and the Private* (London: Heinemann, 1983) p. 20.
21. Hebditch and Anning, *Porn Gold*, p. 53.
22. Canadian National Survey, II, 1268, quoted in Valverde, *Pornography*, p. 150.
23. Hebditch and Anning, *Porn Gold*, pp. 36–8.
24. Karl Marx, *Das Kapital*, trans. *Capital*, Vol. 1 (London: Lawrence and Wishart, 1947).

Chapter 8: Kappeler and Representation

1. Susanne Kappeler, *The Pornography of Representation*, pp. 52, 53.
2. Ibid., p. 14.
3. Ibid., p. 7 .
4. Ibid., p. 53, p. 95.
5. Ibid., p. 66.
6. Dale Spender, *Man Made Language*.
7. Kappeler, *Representation*, p. 45.
8. John Berger, *Ways of Seeing* (Harmondsworth: Penguin, 1972) p. 47, quoted in Kappeler, *Representation*, p. 45.
9. Aslak Aarhus and Ole Bernt Frosenbaug, 'A Murder in Namibia', *Guardian Weekly*, 8 January 1984, p. 7, quoted in Kappeler, *Representation*, p. 5.
10. Kappeler, *Representation*.
11. Immanuel Kant, 'Critique of Judgement' in William Hardy and Max Westbrook (eds), *Twentieth-Century Criticism: The Major Statements*, trans. J. C. Meredith (New York: The Free Press, 1974) p. 12, quoted in Kappeler, *Representation*, p. 54.
12. Kappeler, *Representation*, p. 57.
13. Ibid., p. 141.
14. Ibid., pp. 142–3.
15. See e.g . ibid., p. 44.
16. Ibid., p. 53.
17. Deirdre English, 'The Politics of Porn: Can Feminists Walk the Line?', *Mother Jones*, 20 April 1980, quoted in Kappeler, *Representation*, p. 44.
18. Marianne Valverde, *Sex, Power and Pleasure*, p. 127.
19. Kappeler, *Representation*, p. 212.
20. G.W.F. Hegel, 'Self Consciousness' in *The Phenomenology of Mind*, trans. A.V. Miller (Oxford: Oxford University Press, 1977) p. 104.

21. Kappeler, *Representation*, p. 53.

Chapter 9: Romantic Fiction: Porn for Women

1. Peter de Mann, Report for Mills and Boon Ltd, *The Romantic Novel: A Survey of Reading Habits*, 1969.
2. See, for example, Janice Radway, *Reading the Romance: Women, Patriarchy and Popular Literature*, (Durham: University of North Carolina Press, 1986) and Jean Radford (ed.), *The Progress of Romance: The Politics of Popular Fiction* (London and New York: Routledge & Kegan Paul, 1986). For a survey of the critical literature, see Alison Assiter, 'Romantic Fiction' in Roman Iwashkin (ed.), *Popular Culture* (Basingstoke: Greenwood Press, forthcoming 1989).
3. See Ann Snitow, 'Mass Market Romance: Porn for Women is Different', *Radical History Review*, No. 20 (1979), reprinted in Ann Snitow, Christine Stansell and Sharon Thompson (eds), *Desire: The Politics of Sexuality* (London: Virago, 1984); see also Marion Bower, 'Daring to Speak its Name: The Relationship of Women to Pornography', *Feminist Review*, No. 24 (Autumn 1986): and Marianne Valverde, *Sex, Power and Pleasure*.
4. See Ann Douglas, 'Soft Porn Culture', *The New Republic*, 30 August 1980.
5. Janice Radway, 'Women Read the Romance', *Feminist Studies*, Vol. 9, No. 1, (Spring 1983).
6. Sara Craven, *Counterfeit Bride* (London: Mills & Boon, 1982) p. 24.
7. Sally Wentworth, *Backfire* (London: Mills & Boon, 1983).
8. Information sent out to prospective writers by Mills & Boon.
9. Essie Summers, *A Lamp for Jonathan* (London: Mills & Boon, 1980).
10. Anne Hampson, *Isle of the Rainbows* (London: Mills & Boon, 1979).
11. David Margolies, 'Mills & Boon, Guilt without Sex', *Red Letters*, No. 14 (Winter 82–3).
12. Tania Modelski, 'The Disappearing Act: A Study of Harlequin Romances', *Signs*, Vol. 5, No. 1 (1980).
13. Ann Snitow, *Mass Market Romance*, pp. 259–60.
14. Janet Bailey, *Strange Bedfellow* (London: Mills & Boon, 1979), p. 164.
15. D. H. Lawrence, *Lady Chatterley's Lover* (New York: New American Library, 1959) p. 231.
16. Ibid., p. 17.
17. Ann Snitow, 'Mass Market Romance', p. 265.
18. Anne Hampson, *Isle of the Rainbows*.
19. Ibid., p. 14.
20. Violet Winspear, *The Girl Possessed* (London: Mills & Boon, 1982) p. 10.
21. Sara Craven, *Unguarded Moment* (London: Mills & Boon, 1982).
22. Jack Thomas, quoted in Susan Griffin, *Porn and Silence* (London: The

Women's Press, 1982) p. 61.
23. Anne Hampson, *Isle of the Rainbows*, p. 188.
24. Ibid., p. 16.
25. Essie Summers, *A Lamp for Jonathan*, p. 11.
26. Barbara Cartland, *The Runaway Star* (London: Pan Books, 1961).
27. Marianne Valverde, *Sex, Power and Pleasure*, p. 136.
28. Rosalind Coward, 'What is Porn?' in *Spare Rib*, No. 119 (June 1982) pp. 52–3.
29. Hebditch and Anning, *Porn Gold*, p. 101.
30. Germaine Greer, *The Female Eunuch*, (London: Paladin, 1970).
31. Beatrix Faust, *Women, Sex and Pornography* (Harmondsworth: Penguin, 1982).
32. Maria Marcus, *A Taste for Pain, On Masochism and Female Sexuality* (London: Condor Books, 1978).
33. Marion Bower, 'Daring to Speak its Name: the Relationship of Women to Pornography', *Feminist Review*, No. 24 (Autumn 1986).
34. David Margolies, 'Guilt without Sex'.
35. See, for example, Ann Snitow, 'Mass Market Romance'; Rosalind Coward, *Female Desire: Women's Sexuality Today* (London: Paladin, 1984); and Tania Modelski, 'The Disappearing Act: A Study of Harlequin Romances'.
36. Alison Light, 'Return to Manderley – Romance Fiction, Female Sexuality and Class', *Feminist Review*, No. 16 (Summer 1984).
37. Marion Bower, 'Daring to Speak its Name'.

Chapter 10: Porn and Autonomy

1. Pauline Reage, *The Story of O*, trans. Sabina d'Estrée (New York: Grove, 1965) p. 16.
2. Ibid., p. 113.
3. Georges Bataille, *Eroticism* (London and New York: Marian Boyars, 1987) p. 167.
4. Ibid., p. 177.
5. G.W.F. Hegel, *The Phenomenology of Mind*.
6. Ibid., p. 229.
7. See, for example, Irving Singer, *The Goals of Human Sexuality* (New York: Norton, 1973).
8. Donald Symons, *The Evolution of Human Sexuality* (Oxford: Oxford University Press, 1979) p. 181.
9. Jessica Benjamin, 'Master and Slave: The Fantasy of Erotic Domination', in Ann Snitow et al. (eds), *Desire: The Politics of Sexuality*, pp. 292–312.
10. Ibid., p. 296.
11. Ibid., p. 303.

12. Ibid., p. 303.
13. Ibid., p. 306.
14. Michael Goldstein and Harold Kant, *Porn and Sexual Deviance* (Berkeley: University of California Press, 1973) pp. 135–6.
15. Susan Barrowclough, 'Review of "Not a Love Story"', *Screen*, Vol. 23, No. 5, (1982) pp. 26–36.
16. See George Sterner, in David Holbrook (ed.), *The Case Against Pornography* (La Salle: Open Court, 1973) pp. 227–36.
17. Kenneth Tynan, 'Dirty Books can Stay' in Douglas A. Hughes (ed.), *Perspectives on Pornography*.
18. See Galvin Pollack, 'Pornography: A Trip Around the World', in Douglas A. Hughes (ed.), ibid.
19. Christopher Cherry 'When is Fantasising Morally Bad?', *Philosophical Review*, Vol. 8 (1987) pp. 109–57.
20. C. Cherry, quoting Lynne Segal, 'Sensual Uncertainty, or why the Clitoris is not Enough', in Ryan and Cartledge (eds.), *Sex and Love*, pp. 42–3.
21. Ibid.
22. Andy Moye, 'Pornography'.
23. Richard Wollheim, 'A Charismatic View of Porn', *New York Review of Books*, Vol. 27.
24. Beverly Brown, 'A Feminist Interest in Porn: Some Modest Proposals', *m/f*, No. 5/6 (1981).
25. See Chapter 5.
26. Susan L. Fagin, 'Some Pleasures of the Imagination', *Journal of Aesthetics and Art Criticism*, Vol. 1, No. 43 (1984) pp. 41–55.
27. See Angela Carter, *The Sadean Women* (London: Virago, 1979) p. 16.
28. Plato, *Phaedrus*, ed. by R. Hackforth (Cambridge: Cambridge University Press, 1972).
29. Rene Descartes, *Dioptrics*.
30. Keller in *Discovering Reality*.
31. William Bridgman in 'Porn as a Political Expression' (*Journal of Popular Culture*, 17, 2, [1983] pp. 129–34) argues that porn expresses a philosophical viewpoint of naturalism. Although I wouldn't go quite so far as to suggest that porn 'expresses' a philosophical viewpoint, I do believe that it reflects one.
32. T. Adorno and M. Horkhemer, *Dialectic of Enlightenment* (London: Verso, 1979).
33. Ibid., p. 13.
34. Ibid., p. 29.
35. Ibid., p. 29.
36. Ibid., p. 34.
37. Ibid., p. 34.

38. Ibid., p. 39.
39. Nietzsche, *Transvaluation of all Values*, Vol. VIII (Kramer, Werke) p. 218.
40. *Juliette*, Vol. l, p. 315f, quoted in Adorno, *Dialectic of Enlightenment*, p. 97.

Conclusion

1. See Megan Boler et al., 'We Sisters Join Together' in Lederer (ed.), *Take Back the Night*, p. 263.
2. London Revolutionary Feminist (Anti-Porn) Group, 'Pornography' in Dusty Rhodes and Sandra McNeill, *Women Against Violence Against Women*, p. 15.
3. Andrea Dworkin, 'For Men, Freedom of Speech for Women, Silence Please' in Lederer (ed.), *Take Back the Night*, pp. 255–6.
4. Martha Gever and Marg Hall, 'Fighting Pornography', in Lederer (ed.), *Take Back the Night*, p. 280.
5. There is an extensive literature (mostly American) on this subject, and I do not have the space to cover all the arguments here. The arguments range from 'goals-based' and 'rights-based' liberal ones to new morality and feminist ones. See, for example, Fred Berger, 'Pornography, Feminism, and Censorship', in C. Baker and F. Elliston (eds), *Philosophy and Sex* (Buffalo: Prometheus, 1984); Walter Berns, 'Porn vs Democracy: The Case for Censorship', *Pornography, The Public Interest*, 22 Winter 1971, pp. 25–44; Ronald Dworkin, 'Is There a Right to Porn?' *Oxford Journal of Legal Studies*, 1 (1981), reprinted in Ronald Dworkin, *A Matter of Principle* (Oxford: Oxford University Press, 1986); David Copp and Susan Wendell (eds), *Porn and Censorship* (Buffalo: Prometheus, 1983); Judith Wager Decew, 'Violent Porn: Censorship Morality and Social Alternatives', *Journal of Applied Philosophy*, Vol. 1, No 1, (1984), pp. 79–94; Lester A. Sobel (ed), *Pornography, Obscenity and the Law* (New York: Facts on File, 1979).
6. Valverde, *Sex, Power and Pleasure*, p. 122.
7. Robin Morgan, 'Theory and Practice: Pornography and Rape' in *Take Back the Night*, p. 128.
8. Valverde, *Sex, Power and Pleasure*, p. 143.
9. See ibid., p. 127
10. For an analysis of the variety of meanings attaching to visual representations, particularly pornographic imagery, see Rosalind Coward, 'Sexual Violence and Sexuality', *Feminist Review* (Summer 1982) pp. 9–22.

Index